I0355551

TEACHER'S PET PUBLICATIONS

PUZZLE PACK
for
A Raisin in the Sun

based on the play by
Lorriane Hansberry

Written by
William T. Collins

INTRODUCTION

If you already own the LitPlan for this title, this Puzzle Pack will refresh your Unit Resource Materials and Vocabulary Resource Materials sections plus give you additional materials you can substitute into the tests.If you do not already have a complete LitPlan, these pages will give you some supplemental materials to use with your own plan. There are two main groups of materials: one set for unit words (such as characters' names, symbols, places, etc.) and one set for vocabulary words associated with the book.

WORD LIST

There is a word list for both the unit words and the vocabulary words. These lists show you which words are being used in the materials and the clues or definitions being used for those words. You may want to give students a word list with clues/definitions to help them, or you may want students to only have a word list (without clues/definitions) if you want them to work a little harder. Both are available for duplication. The word lists can also be your "calling key" for the bingo games.

FILL IN THE BLANK AND MATCHING

There are 4 each of the fill in the blank and matching worksheets for both the unit and vocabulary words. These pages can be used either as extra worksheets for students or as objective parts of a unit test. They can be done individually if students need extra help or as a whole class activity to review the material covered.

MAGIC SQUARES

The magic squares not only reinforce the material covered but also work on reasoning and math skills. Many teachers have told us that their students really enjoy doing these!

WORD SEARCH PUZZLES

The word search words go in all directions, as indicated on your answer keys. Two of the word search puzzles have the clues listed rather than the words. This makes the puzzle a little more difficult, but it reinforces the material better. Two word search puzzles have words only for students who find the clue puzzles too difficult.

CROSSWORD PUZZLES

Both unit and vocabulary word sections have 4 crossword puzzles.

BINGO CARDS

There are 32 individual bingo cards for the unit words and 32 individual bingo cards for the vocabulary words. You can use your word list as a "call list," calling the words at random and marking them off of your list as you go, or you could use the flash cards by cutting them apart and drawing the words at random from a hat (or box or whatever). To make a better review, you might ask for the definition and spelling of each word as you call it out–or you could call out the definitions and have students tell you the words they need to look for on the puzzle.

JUGGLE LETTERS

The vocabulary juggle letter game is intended to help students learn the spellings of the words. One sheet has the definitions listed on it as an extra help for students who need it or to reinforce the definitions if you choose to do so.

FLASH CARDS

We've included a set of vocabulary flash cards you can duplicate, cut, and fold for your students. Some teachers make a few sets for general use by the class; others make a set for each student. Some teachers duplicate them for each student and have the students cut & fold their own. You can cut out just the words and put them in a hat, have each student pick out one word and write the definition and a sentence for that word. Students then swap words and papers, with the next student adding a sentence of his own under the last one. You can have students swap as many times as you like. Each time the student will read the sentences written prior to his own and then add a sentence. You can cut out the words and definitions separately and play "I Have; Who Has?" Each student in the room draws a word and definition. The first student says, "I have (the name of the word). Who has the definition?" The student with the definition reads it then says, "I have (the name of the vocabulary word she has). Who has the definition?" The round continues until all words and definitions have been given.

A Raisin in the Sun Unit Word List

No.	Word	Clue/Definition
1.	ACT	Play division
2.	AFRICA	Asagai's home continent
3.	ALAIYO	One For Whom Bread-Food-Is Not Enough
4.	ASAGAI	Beneatha's African intellectual boyfriend
5.	ASSIMILATIONIST	Someone who is willing to give up his own culture and submerge himself in the dominant ...culture.
6.	BABY	Ruth was going to have one
7.	BENEATHA	Walter's sister
8.	BOBO	He brought Walter bad news about the money
9.	BRIBE	Pay-off; illegal money
10.	CHECK	Financial document made payable to Mama
11.	CHICAGO	City where Walter and Ruth live
12.	CLYBOURNE	_______ Park
13.	DOCTOR	What Beneatha wanted to study to be
14.	DROVE	What Walter did on his day(s) away from work
15.	EDUCATION	Schooling
16.	EGGS	Damn all the _______ that ever was!
17.	GEORGE	Beneatha wouldn't marry him because he was shallow
18.	GOD	Beneatha did not believe in Him
19.	HANSBERRY	Author
20.	HAT	Travis's present to Mama
21.	IDEALISTS	Those who see the changes in the long line of life
22.	INSURANCE	Source of Mama's money
23.	IRON	Ruth did it to the clothes
24.	LINDNER	Representative from the Clybourne Park Improvement Assoc.
25.	LIQUOR	Kind of store Walter wants to buy
26.	MAMA	Walter's mother
27.	MAN	I tell you I am a __________!!
28.	MARRY	Asagai asked Beneatha to _______ him.
29.	MONEY	Dollars
30.	NIGERIA	Asagai's home county
31.	PEARLS	Walter though his wife should wear some ______ in this world.
32.	PLANT	Last thing Mama takes from the apartment
33.	PREGNANT	Ruth's with child condition
34.	RAISIN	A __________ in the Sun
35.	REALISTS	Those who cannot see the changes or refuse to think
36.	RUTH	Walter's wife
37.	SCENE	Act division
38.	SCHOOL	Mama wanted to set money aside for Beneatha's
39.	TOOLS	Mama got garden __________.
40.	TRAVIS	Walter's son
41.	WALTER	He wanted to get more from life for himself and his family
42.	WILLY	He ran off with the liquor store money
43.	WORK	Daily job

A Raisin in the Sun Fill In The Blank 1

_______________ 1. Author

_______________ 2. What Beneatha wanted to study to be

_______________ 3. Travis's present to Mama

_______________ 4. Beneatha wouldn't marry him because he was shallow

_______________ 5. Dollars

_______________ 6. Ruth did it to the clothes

_______________ 7. Ruth's with child condition

_______________ 8. Someone who is willing to give up his own culture and submerge himself in the dominant ...culture.

_______________ 9. Daily job

_______________ 10. One For Whom Bread-Food-Is Not Enough

_______________ 11. I tell you I am a __________!!

_______________ 12. Walter though his wife should wear some ______ in this world.

_______________ 13. Last thing Mama takes from the apartment

_______________ 14. Schooling

_______________ 15. Pay-off; illegal money

_______________ 16. Those who cannot see the changes or refuse to think

_______________ 17. Walter's sister

_______________ 18. Source of Mama's money

_______________ 19. He ran off with the liquor store money

_______________ 20. Beneatha's African intellectual boyfriend

A Raisin in the Sun Fill In The Blank 1 Answer Key

HANSBERRY	1. Author
DOCTOR	2. What Beneatha wanted to study to be
HAT	3. Travis's present to Mama
GEORGE	4. Beneatha wouldn't marry him because he was shallow
MONEY	5. Dollars
IRON	6. Ruth did it to the clothes
PREGNANT	7. Ruth's with child condition
ASSIMILATIONIST	8. Someone who is willing to give up his own culture and submerge himself in the dominant ...culture.
WORK	9. Daily job
ALAIYO	10. One For Whom Bread-Food-Is Not Enough
MAN	11. I tell you I am a __________!!
PEARLS	12. Walter though his wife should wear some ______ in this world.
PLANT	13. Last thing Mama takes from the apartment
EDUCATION	14. Schooling
BRIBE	15. Pay-off; illegal money
REALISTS	16. Those who cannot see the changes or refuse to think
BENEATHA	17. Walter's sister
INSURANCE	18. Source of Mama's money
WILLY	19. He ran off with the liquor store money
ASAGAI	20. Beneatha's African intellectual boyfriend

A Raisin in the Sun Fill In The Blank 2

1. He ran off with the liquor store money
2. _______ Park
3. Mama wanted to set money aside for Beneatha's
4. Ruth was going to have one
5. Asagai's home county
6. Source of Mama's money
7. Those who see the changes in the long line of life
8. City where Walter and Ruth live
9. He wanted to get more from life for himself and his family
10. What Walter did on his day(s) away from work
11. Author
12. Ruth's with child condition
13. Kind of store Walter wants to buy
14. Schooling
15. Representative from the Clybourne Park Improvement Assoc.
16. Play division
17. Asagai asked Beneatha to _______ him.
18. Mama got garden __________.
19. Beneatha's African intellectual boyfriend
20. What Beneatha wanted to study to be

A Raisin in the Sun Fill In The Blank 2 Answer Key

WILLY	1.	He ran off with the liquor store money
CLYBOURNE	2.	_______ Park
SCHOOL	3.	Mama wanted to set money aside for Beneatha's
BABY	4.	Ruth was going to have one
NIGERIA	5.	Asagai's home county
INSURANCE	6.	Source of Mama's money
IDEALISTS	7.	Those who see the changes in the long line of life
CHICAGO	8.	City where Walter and Ruth live
WALTER	9.	He wanted to get more from life for himself and his family
DROVE	10.	What Walter did on his day(s) away from work
HANSBERRY	11.	Author
PREGNANT	12.	Ruth's with child condition
LIQUOR	13.	Kind of store Walter wants to buy
EDUCATION	14.	Schooling
LINDNER	15.	Representative from the Clybourne Park Improvement Assoc.
ACT	16.	Play division
MARRY	17.	Asagai asked Beneatha to _______ him.
TOOLS	18.	Mama got garden __________.
ASAGAI	19.	Beneatha's African intellectual boyfriend
DOCTOR	20.	What Beneatha wanted to study to be

A Raisin in the Sun Fill In The Blank 3

________________ 1. City where Walter and Ruth live

________________ 2. Last thing Mama takes from the apartment

________________ 3. I tell you I am a __________!!

________________ 4. He brought Walter bad news about the money

________________ 5. Financial document made payable to Mama

________________ 6. He wanted to get more from life for himself and his family

________________ 7. Source of Mama's money

________________ 8. Dollars

________________ 9. Walter though his wife should wear some ______ in this world.

________________ 10. Play division

________________ 11. Walter's mother

________________ 12. He ran off with the liquor store money

________________ 13. Pay-off; illegal money

________________ 14. Ruth did it to the clothes

________________ 15. Those who see the changes in the long line of life

________________ 16. Author

________________ 17. Ruth was going to have one

________________ 18. What Walter did on his day(s) away from work

________________ 19. Daily job

________________ 20. Travis's present to Mama

A Raisin in the Sun Fill In The Blank 3 Answer Key

CHICAGO	1. City where Walter and Ruth live
PLANT	2. Last thing Mama takes from the apartment
MAN	3. I tell you I am a __________!!
BOBO	4. He brought Walter bad news about the money
CHECK	5. Financial document made payable to Mama
WALTER	6. He wanted to get more from life for himself and his family
INSURANCE	7. Source of Mama's money
MONEY	8. Dollars
PEARLS	9. Walter though his wife should wear some ______ in this world.
ACT	10. Play division
MAMA	11. Walter's mother
WILLY	12. He ran off with the liquor store money
BRIBE	13. Pay-off; illegal money
IRON	14. Ruth did it to the clothes
IDEALISTS	15. Those who see the changes in the long line of life
HANSBERRY	16. Author
BABY	17. Ruth was going to have one
DROVE	18. What Walter did on his day(s) away from work
WORK	19. Daily job
HAT	20. Travis's present to Mama

A Raisin in the Sun Fill In The Blank 4

1. Asagai asked Beneatha to _______ him.
2. Walter's sister
3. Walter's mother
4. City where Walter and Ruth live
5. Walter though his wife should wear some ______ in this world.
6. Play division
7. Asagai's home continent
8. Beneatha did not believe in Him
9. Those who see the changes in the long line of life
10. Last thing Mama takes from the apartment
11. Asagai's home county
12. What Beneatha wanted to study to be
13. Financial document made payable to Mama
14. A __________ in the Sun
15. I tell you I am a __________!!
16. Ruth was going to have one
17. Travis's present to Mama
18. He ran off with the liquor store money
19. Daily job
20. Kind of store Walter wants to buy

A Raisin In The Sun Fill In The Blank 4 Answer Key

MARRY	1. Asagai asked Beneatha to _______ him.
BENEATHA	2. Walter's sister
MAMA	3. Walter's mother
CHICAGO	4. City where Walter and Ruth live
PEARLS	5. Walter though his wife should wear some ______ in this world.
ACT	6. Play division
AFRICA	7. Asagai's home continent
GOD	8. Beneatha did not believe in Him
IDEALISTS	9. Those who see the changes in the long line of life
PLANT	10. Last thing Mama takes from the apartment
NIGERIA	11. Asagai's home county
DOCTOR	12. What Beneatha wanted to study to be
CHECK	13. Financial document made payable to Mama
RAISIN	14. A __________ in the Sun
MAN	15. I tell you I am a __________!!
BABY	16. Ruth was going to have one
HAT	17. Travis's present to Mama
WILLY	18. He ran off with the liquor store money
WORK	19. Daily job
LIQUOR	20. Kind of store Walter wants to buy

A Raisin in the Sun Matching 1

___ 1. MONEY	A. Mama wanted to set money aside for Beneatha's
___ 2. INSURANCE	B. Walter's mother
___ 3. PEARLS	C. Financial document made payable to Mama
___ 4. NIGERIA	D. What Beneatha wanted to study to be
___ 5. CHECK	E. Beneatha did not believe in Him
___ 6. PREGNANT	F. Beneatha's African intellectual boyfriend
___ 7. ALAIYO	G. Mama got garden __________.
___ 8. GOD	H. Ruth did it to the clothes
___ 9. DOCTOR	I. _______ Park
___10. ASAGAI	J. Kind of store Walter wants to buy
___11. REALISTS	K. Source of Mama's money
___12. MAMA	L. Beneatha wouldn't marry him because he was shallow
___13. SCHOOL	M. Dollars
___14. GEORGE	N. Ruth's with child condition
___15. LIQUOR	O. Damn all the _______ that ever was!
___16. MAN	P. Play division
___17. TOOLS	Q. I tell you I am a __________!!
___18. CLYBOURNE	R. One For Whom Bread-Food-Is Not Enough
___19. CHICAGO	S. City where Walter and Ruth live
___20. WORK	T. Walter though his wife should wear some ______ in this world.
___21. IRON	U. Walter's wife
___22. RUTH	V. Daily job
___23. EGGS	W. Those who cannot see the changes or refuse to think
___24. BRIBE	X. Asagai's home county
___25. ACT	Y. Pay-off; illegal money

A Raisin in the Sun Matching 1 Answer Key

M - 1. MONEY	A. Mama wanted to set money aside for Beneatha's
K - 2. INSURANCE	B. Walter's mother
T - 3. PEARLS	C. Financial document made payable to Mama
X - 4. NIGERIA	D. What Beneatha wanted to study to be
C - 5. CHECK	E. Beneatha did not believe in Him
N - 6. PREGNANT	F. Beneatha's African intellectual boyfriend
R - 7. ALAIYO	G. Mama got garden __________.
E - 8. GOD	H. Ruth did it to the clothes
D - 9. DOCTOR	I. _______ Park
F - 10. ASAGAI	J. Kind of store Walter wants to buy
W -11. REALISTS	K. Source of Mama's money
B - 12. MAMA	L. Beneatha wouldn't marry him because he was shallow
A - 13. SCHOOL	M. Dollars
L - 14. GEORGE	N. Ruth's with child condition
J - 15. LIQUOR	O. Damn all the _______ that ever was!
Q - 16. MAN	P. Play division
G - 17. TOOLS	Q. I tell you I am a __________!!
I - 18. CLYBOURNE	R. One For Whom Bread-Food-Is Not Enough
S - 19. CHICAGO	S. City where Walter and Ruth live
V - 20. WORK	T. Walter though his wife should wear some ______ in this world.
H - 21. IRON	U. Walter's wife
U - 22. RUTH	V. Daily job
O - 23. EGGS	W. Those who cannot see the changes or refuse to think
Y - 24. BRIBE	X. Asagai's home county
P - 25. ACT	Y. Pay-off; illegal money

A Raisin in the Sun Matching 2

___ 1. WALTER	A. Ruth's with child condition
___ 2. HANSBERRY	B. I tell you I am a __________!!
___ 3. BABY	C. Daily job
___ 4. IRON	D. Damn all the _______ that ever was!
___ 5. MAN	E. He wanted to get more from life for himself and his family
___ 6. WORK	F. Kind of store Walter wants to buy
___ 7. LIQUOR	G. Mama got garden __________.
___ 8. PEARLS	H. Those who see the changes in the long line of life
___ 9. TOOLS	I. Financial document made payable to Mama
___10. EGGS	J. Source of Mama's money
___11. HAT	K. Asagai's home continent
___12. MAMA	L. Walter's mother
___13. GOD	M. Last thing Mama takes from the apartment
___14. MARRY	N. Play division
___15. CHECK	O. Ruth was going to have one
___16. DOCTOR	P. Asagai asked Beneatha to _______ him.
___17. PLANT	Q. Beneatha did not believe in Him
___18. MONEY	R. Walter's wife
___19. RUTH	S. Travis's present to Mama
___20. PREGNANT	T. Dollars
___21. IDEALISTS	U. Author
___22. ACT	V. Asagai's home county
___23. NIGERIA	W. Walter though his wife should wear some ______ in this world.
___24. AFRICA	X. Ruth did it to the clothes
___25. INSURANCE	Y. What Beneatha wanted to study to be

A Raisin in the Sun Matching 2 Answer Key

E - 1.	WALTER	A. Ruth's with child condition
U - 2.	HANSBERRY	B. I tell you I am a __________!!
O - 3.	BABY	C. Daily job
X - 4.	IRON	D. Damn all the _______ that ever was!
B - 5.	MAN	E. He wanted to get more from life for himself and his family
C - 6.	WORK	F. Kind of store Walter wants to buy
F - 7.	LIQUOR	G. Mama got garden __________.
W - 8.	PEARLS	H. Those who see the changes in the long line of life
G - 9.	TOOLS	I. Financial document made payable to Mama
D -10.	EGGS	J. Source of Mama's money
S -11.	HAT	K. Asagai's home continent
L - 12.	MAMA	L. Walter's mother
Q -13.	GOD	M. Last thing Mama takes from the apartment
P -14.	MARRY	N. Play division
I - 15.	CHECK	O. Ruth was going to have one
Y -16.	DOCTOR	P. Asagai asked Beneatha to _______ him.
M -17.	PLANT	Q. Beneatha did not believe in Him
T - 18.	MONEY	R. Walter's wife
R -19.	RUTH	S. Travis's present to Mama
A -20.	PREGNANT	T. Dollars
H -21.	IDEALISTS	U. Author
N -22.	ACT	V. Asagai's home county
V -23.	NIGERIA	W. Walter though his wife should wear some ______ in this world.
K -24.	AFRICA	X. Ruth did it to the clothes
J - 25.	INSURANCE	Y. What Beneatha wanted to study to be

A Raisin in the Sun Matching 3

___ 1. WILLY	A. Beneatha wouldn't marry him because he was shallow
___ 2. RUTH	B. Author
___ 3. ACT	C. Ruth did it to the clothes
___ 4. PREGNANT	D. Mama got garden ___________.
___ 5. DOCTOR	E. Walter's wife
___ 6. NIGERIA	F. What Beneatha wanted to study to be
___ 7. WORK	G. Asagai's home county
___ 8. IDEALISTS	H. Pay-off; illegal money
___ 9. MAMA	I. Daily job
___10. BRIBE	J. Last thing Mama takes from the apartment
___11. SCENE	K. Walter's sister
___12. GEORGE	L. Those who see the changes in the long line of life
___13. BENEATHA	M. Act division
___14. DROVE	N. Play division
___15. GOD	O. He ran off with the liquor store money
___16. MONEY	P. Asagai's home continent
___17. PLANT	Q. Dollars
___18. INSURANCE	R. ________ Park
___19. TOOLS	S. Ruth's with child condition
___20. CLYBOURNE	T. He wanted to get more from life for himself and his family
___21. HANSBERRY	U. One For Whom Bread-Food-Is Not Enough
___22. WALTER	V. What Walter did on his day(s) away from work
___23. IRON	W. Walter's mother
___24. AFRICA	X. Source of Mama's money
___25. ALAIYO	Y. Beneatha did not believe in Him

A Raisin in the Sun Matching 3 Answer Key

O - 1. WILLY	A. Beneatha wouldn't marry him because he was shallow
E - 2. RUTH	B. Author
N - 3. ACT	C. Ruth did it to the clothes
S - 4. PREGNANT	D. Mama got garden __________.
F - 5. DOCTOR	E. Walter's wife
G - 6. NIGERIA	F. What Beneatha wanted to study to be
I - 7. WORK	G. Asagai's home county
L - 8. IDEALISTS	H. Pay-off; illegal money
W - 9. MAMA	I. Daily job
H -10. BRIBE	J. Last thing Mama takes from the apartment
M -11. SCENE	K. Walter's sister
A -12. GEORGE	L. Those who see the changes in the long line of life
K -13. BENEATHA	M. Act division
V -14. DROVE	N. Play division
Y -15. GOD	O. He ran off with the liquor store money
Q -16. MONEY	P. Asagai's home continent
J - 17. PLANT	Q. Dollars
X -18. INSURANCE	R. _______ Park
D -19. TOOLS	S. Ruth's with child condition
R -20. CLYBOURNE	T. He wanted to get more from life for himself and his family
B -21. HANSBERRY	U. One For Whom Bread-Food-Is Not Enough
T -22. WALTER	V. What Walter did on his day(s) away from work
C -23. IRON	W. Walter's mother
P -24. AFRICA	X. Source of Mama's money
U -25. ALAIYO	Y. Beneatha did not believe in Him

A Raisin in the Sun Matching 4

___ 1. EGGS	A. Ruth did it to the clothes
___ 2. CHICAGO	B. Those who see the changes in the long line of life
___ 3. MAMA	C. Someone who is willing to give up his own culture and submerge himself in the dominant ...culture.
___ 4. BRIBE	D. Author
___ 5. TRAVIS	E. Ruth was going to have one
___ 6. HANSBERRY	F. Walter's son
___ 7. DOCTOR	G. Those who cannot see the changes or refuse to think
___ 8. REALISTS	H. Walter's sister
___ 9. MARRY	I. What Beneatha wanted to study to be
___10. BENEATHA	J. Representative from the Clybourne Park Improvement Assoc.
___11. IRON	K. Asagai's home county
___12. LINDNER	L. Damn all the _______ that ever was!
___13. PREGNANT	M. Walter though his wife should wear some ______ in this world.
___14. WILLY	N. One For Whom Bread-Food-Is Not Enough
___15. SCENE	O. Act division
___16. RUTH	P. Walter's wife
___17. ALAIYO	Q. He wanted to get more from life for himself and his family
___18. WALTER	R. Dollars
___19. ASSIMILATIONIST	S. Pay-off; illegal money
___20. IDEALISTS	T. Walter's mother
___21. MONEY	U. Source of Mama's money
___22. INSURANCE	V. Ruth's with child condition
___23. PEARLS	W. Asagai asked Beneatha to _______ him.
___24. NIGERIA	X. He ran off with the liquor store money
___25. BABY	Y. City where Walter and Ruth live

A Raisin in the Sun Matching 4 Answer Key

L - 1. EGGS	A. Ruth did it to the clothes
Y - 2. CHICAGO	B. Those who see the changes in the long line of life
T - 3. MAMA	C. Someone who is willing to give up his own culture and submerge himself in the dominant ...culture.
S - 4. BRIBE	D. Author
F - 5. TRAVIS	E. Ruth was going to have one
D - 6. HANSBERRY	F. Walter's son
I - 7. DOCTOR	G. Those who cannot see the changes or refuse to think
G - 8. REALISTS	H. Walter's sister
W - 9. MARRY	I. What Beneatha wanted to study to be
H -10. BENEATHA	J. Representative from the Clybourne Park Improvement Assoc.
A -11. IRON	K. Asagai's home county
J - 12. LINDNER	L. Damn all the _______ that ever was!
V -13. PREGNANT	M. Walter though his wife should wear some ______ in this world.
X -14. WILLY	N. One For Whom Bread-Food-Is Not Enough
O -15. SCENE	O. Act division
P -16. RUTH	P. Walter's wife
N -17. ALAIYO	Q. He wanted to get more from life for himself and his family
Q -18. WALTER	R. Dollars
C -19. ASSIMILATIONIST	S. Pay-off; illegal money
B -20. IDEALISTS	T. Walter's mother
R -21. MONEY	U. Source of Mama's money
U -22. INSURANCE	V. Ruth's with child condition
M -23. PEARLS	W. Asagai asked Beneatha to _______ him.
K -24. NIGERIA	X. He ran off with the liquor store money
E -25. BABY	Y. City where Walter and Ruth live

A Raisin in the Sun Magic Squares 1

Match the definition with the vocabulary word. Put your answers in the magic squares below. When your answers are correct, all columns and rows will add to the same number.

A. HAT
B. MAMA
C. IRON
D. BRIBE
E. GOD
F. EGGS
G. IDEALISTS
H. TOOLS
I. BABY
J. BENEATHA
K. SCHOOL
L. MONEY
M. RUTH
N. ACT
O. MAN
P. PLANT

1. Mama got garden ___________.
2. Walter's wife
3. Walter's mother
4. Mama wanted to set money aside for Beneatha's
5. Walter's sister
6. Ruth did it to the clothes
7. Last thing Mama takes from the apartment
8. Beneatha did not believe in Him
9. I tell you I am a __________!!
10. Damn all the _______ that ever was!
11. Ruth was going to have one
12. Pay-off; illegal money
13. Travis's present to Mama
14. Dollars
15. Those who see the changes in the long line of life
16. Play division

A=	B=	C=	D=
E=	F=	G=	H=
I=	J=	K=	L=
M=	N=	O=	P=

A Raisin in the Sun Magic Squares 1 Answer Key

Match the definition with the vocabulary word. Put your answers in the magic squares below. When your answers are correct, all columns and rows will add to the same number.

A. HAT
B. MAMA
C. IRON
D. BRIBE
E. GOD
F. EGGS

G. IDEALISTS
H. TOOLS
I. BABY
J. BENEATHA
K. SCHOOL
L. MONEY

M. RUTH
N. ACT
O. MAN
P. PLANT

1. Mama got garden ___________.
2. Walter's wife
3. Walter's mother
4. Mama wanted to set money aside for Beneatha's
5. Walter's sister
6. Ruth did it to the clothes
7. Last thing Mama takes from the apartment
8. Beneatha did not believe in Him
9. I tell you I am a ___________!!
10. Damn all the ________ that ever was!
11. Ruth was going to have one
12. Pay-off; illegal money
13. Travis's present to Mama
14. Dollars
15. Those who see the changes in the long line of life
16. Play division

A=13	B=3	C=6	D=12
E=8	F=10	G=15	H=1
I=11	J=5	K=4	L=14
M=2	N=16	O=9	P=7

A Raisin in the Sun Magic Squares 2

Match the definition with the vocabulary word. Put your answers in the magic squares below. When your answers are correct, all columns and rows will add to the same number.

A. GEORGE
B. MARRY
C. ALAIYO
D. IDEALISTS
E. BENEATHA
F. EDUCATION
G. MAN
H. ASSIMILATIONIST
I. MONEY
J. WALTER
K. ASAGAI
L. SCHOOL
M. PLANT
N. BABY
O. HANSBERRY
P. WILLY

1. Author
2. Those who see the changes in the long line of life
3. He wanted to get more from life for himself and his family
4. Walter's sister
5. Dollars
6. Schooling
7. He ran off with the liquor store money
8. One For Whom Bread-Food-Is Not Enough
9. Someone who is willing to give up his own culture and submerge himself in the dominant ...culture.
10. Beneatha's African intellectual boyfriend
11. Beneatha wouldn't marry him because he was shallow
12. Ruth was going to have one
13. Asagai asked Beneatha to _______ him.
14. Last thing Mama takes from the apartment
15. I tell you I am a __________!!
16. Mama wanted to set money aside for Beneatha's

A=	B=	C=	D=
E=	F=	G=	H=
I=	J=	K=	L=
M=	N=	O=	P=

A Raisin in the Sun Magic Squares 2 Answer Key

Match the definition with the vocabulary word. Put your answers in the magic squares below. When your answers are correct, all columns and rows will add to the same number.

A. GEORGE
B. MARRY
C. ALAIYO
D. IDEALISTS
E. BENEATHA
F. EDUCATION
G. MAN
H. ASSIMILATIONIST
I. MONEY
J. WALTER
K. ASAGAI
L. SCHOOL
M. PLANT
N. BABY
O. HANSBERRY
P. WILLY

1. Author
2. Those who see the changes in the long line of life
3. He wanted to get more from life for himself and his family
4. Walter's sister
5. Dollars
6. Schooling
7. He ran off with the liquor store money
8. One For Whom Bread-Food-Is Not Enough
9. Someone who is willing to give up his own culture and submerge himself in the dominant ...culture.
10. Beneatha's African intellectual boyfriend
11. Beneatha wouldn't marry him because he was shallow
12. Ruth was going to have one
13. Asagai asked Beneatha to ________ him.
14. Last thing Mama takes from the apartment
15. I tell you I am a __________!!
16. Mama wanted to set money aside for Beneatha's

A=11	B=13	C=8	D=2
E=4	F=6	G=15	H=9
I=5	J=3	K=10	L=16
M=14	N=12	O=1	P=7

A Raisin in the Sun Magic Squares 3

Match the definition with the vocabulary word. Put your answers in the magic squares below. When your answers are correct, all columns and rows will add to the same number.

A. MAMA
B. GOD
C. NIGERIA
D. ALAIYO
E. CHECK
F. PEARLS
G. CLYBOURNE
H. BENEATHA
I. DOCTOR
J. TRAVIS
K. RAISIN
L. SCHOOL
M. CHICAGO
N. ASAGAI
O. ACT
P. HANSBERRY

1. Walter though his wife should wear some ______ in this world.
2. What Beneatha wanted to study to be
3. Play division
4. One For Whom Bread-Food-Is Not Enough
5. City where Walter and Ruth live
6. Beneatha did not believe in Him
7. Walter's sister
8. A __________ in the Sun
9. Asagai's home county
10. Author
11. Walter's son
12. Financial document made payable to Mama
13. Mama wanted to set money aside for Beneatha's
14. _______ Park
15. Walter's mother
16. Beneatha's African intellectual boyfriend

A=	B=	C=	D=
E=	F=	G=	H=
I=	J=	K=	L=
M=	N=	O=	P=

A Raisin in the Sun Magic Squares 3 Answer Key

Match the definition with the vocabulary word. Put your answers in the magic squares below. When your answers are correct, all columns and rows will add to the same number.

A. MAMA
B. GOD
C. NIGERIA
D. ALAIYO
E. CHECK
F. PEARLS
G. CLYBOURNE
H. BENEATHA
I. DOCTOR
J. TRAVIS
K. RAISIN
L. SCHOOL
M. CHICAGO
N. ASAGAI
O. ACT
P. HANSBERRY

1. Walter though his wife should wear some _______ in this world.
2. What Beneatha wanted to study to be
3. Play division
4. One For Whom Bread-Food-Is Not Enough
5. City where Walter and Ruth live
6. Beneatha did not believe in Him
7. Walter's sister
8. A ___________ in the Sun
9. Asagai's home county
10. Author
11. Walter's son
12. Financial document made payable to Mama
13. Mama wanted to set money aside for Beneatha's
14. ________ Park
15. Walter's mother
16. Beneatha's African intellectual boyfriend

A=15	B=6	C=9	D=4
E=12	F=1	G=14	H=7
I=2	J=11	K=8	L=13
M=5	N=16	O=3	P=10

A Raisin in the Sun Magic Squares 4

Match the definition with the vocabulary word. Put your answers in the magic squares below. When your answers are correct, all columns and rows will add to the same number.

A. BABY
B. MARRY
C. DROVE
D. ACT
E. LINDNER
F. IRON
G. DOCTOR
H. PLANT
I. MAN
J. MONEY
K. PREGNANT
L. ASAGAI
M. HAT
N. GEORGE
O. PEARLS
P. AFRICA

1. Asagai asked Beneatha to _______ him.
2. What Beneatha wanted to study to be
3. Ruth's with child condition
4. Beneatha wouldn't marry him because he was shallow
5. Travis's present to Mama
6. Beneatha's African intellectual boyfriend
7. Last thing Mama takes from the apartment
8. Ruth was going to have one
9. Asagai's home continent
10. I tell you I am a __________!!
11. Representative from the Clybourne Park Improvement Assoc.
12. Play division
13. What Walter did on his day(s) away from work
14. Ruth did it to the clothes
15. Dollars
16. Walter though his wife should wear some ______ in this world.

A=	B=	C=	D=
E=	F=	G=	H=
I=	J=	K=	L=
M=	N=	O=	P=

A Raisin in the Sun Magic Squares 4 Answer Key

Match the definition with the vocabulary word. Put your answers in the magic squares below. When your answers are correct, all columns and rows will add to the same number.

A. BABY
B. MARRY
C. DROVE
D. ACT
E. LINDNER
F. IRON
G. DOCTOR
H. PLANT
I. MAN
J. MONEY
K. PREGNANT
L. ASAGAI
M. HAT
N. GEORGE
O. PEARLS
P. AFRICA

1. Asagai asked Beneatha to _______ him.
2. What Beneatha wanted to study to be
3. Ruth's with child condition
4. Beneatha wouldn't marry him because he was shallow
5. Travis's present to Mama
6. Beneatha's African intellectual boyfriend
7. Last thing Mama takes from the apartment
8. Ruth was going to have one
9. Asagai's home continent
10. I tell you I am a __________!!
11. Representative from the Clybourne Park Improvement Assoc.
12. Play division
13. What Walter did on his day(s) away from work
14. Ruth did it to the clothes
15. Dollars
16. Walter though his wife should wear some ______ in this world.

A=8	B=1	C=13	D=12
E=11	F=14	G=2	H=7
I=10	J=15	K=3	L=6
M=5	N=4	O=16	P=9

A Raisin in the Sun Word Search 1

Words are placed backwards, forward, diagonally, up and down. Clues listed below can help you find the words. Circle the hidden vocabulary words in the maze.

A	L	A	I	Y	O	S	W	B	A	R	A	I	S	I	N	F	G	C
X	D	P	L	N	J	Z	O	I	M	N	U	T	Z	A	O	T	O	Z
J	G	P	R	I	Q	P	R	N	A	P	S	T	M	G	R	Y	D	G
G	P	N	R	R	N	E	K	J	M	I	M	R	H	A	I	H	O	L
T	O	O	L	S	G	D	V	X	L	O	O	H	C	S	G	G	E	P
N	R	F	L	I	T	M	N	A	N	U	P	T	L	A	A	N	D	R
A	M	A	N	S	G	A	E	E	Q	P	C	R	D	C	E	G	U	T
N	D	J	V	C	T	R	Y	I	R	H	A	Y	I	C	H	E	C	K
G	J	P	X	I	S	R	L	O	T	E	B	H	S	H	B	O	A	W
E	F	L	T	L	S	Y	T	K	P	A	C	B	D	I	C	R	T	P
R	C	A	F	R	I	C	A	L	B	M	Y	O	R	W	L	G	I	X
P	H	N	Z	L	O	D	C	G	E	F	F	B	H	A	Y	E	O	L
T	A	T	P	D	C	V	T	K	N	Q	N	O	L	L	B	P	N	W
F	N	D	S	T	S	I	L	A	E	D	I	I	T	T	O	D	H	X
L	S	K	F	D	V	F	G	B	A	Q	C	N	Y	E	U	R	G	F
M	B	J	W	H	S	X	P	L	T	S	H	S	S	R	R	O	T	P
M	E	M	N	M	T	B	G	R	H	J	C	U	W	F	N	V	Y	R
L	R	W	I	L	L	Y	D	R	A	G	T	R	V	Z	E	E	N	C
N	R	L	Y	R	Z	N	Y	X	Q	F	T	A	N	Z	N	S	T	V
B	Y	H	K	D	L	L	N	Y	G	K	J	N	M	Y	L	Q	X	J
D	Z	R	L	T	P	N	V	D	Y	V	M	C	T	J	M	T	L	X
G	W	J	B	Y	Y	Z	P	M	W	W	M	E	X	K	X	N	J	S

A __________ in the Sun (6)
Act division (5)
Asagai asked Beneatha to _______ him. (5)
Asagai's home continent (6)
Asagai's home county (7)
Author (9)
Beneatha did not believe in Him (3)
Beneatha wouldn't marry him because he was shallow (6)
Beneatha's African intellectual boyfriend (6)
City where Walter and Ruth live (7)
Daily job (4)
Damn all the _______ that ever was! (4)
Dollars (5)
Financial document made payable to Mama (5)
He brought Walter bad news about the money (4)
He ran off with the liquor store money (5)
He wanted to get more from life for himself and his family (6)
I tell you I am a __________!! (3)
Kind of store Walter wants to buy (6)
Last thing Mama takes from the apartment (5)
Mama got garden __________. (5)
Mama wanted to set money aside for Beneatha's (6)
One For Whom Bread-Food-Is Not Enough (6)
Pay-off; illegal money (5)
Play division (3)
Representative from the Clybourne Park Improvement Assoc. (7)
Ruth did it to the clothes (4)
Ruth was going to have one (4)
Ruth's with child condition (8)
Schooling (9)
Source of Mama's money (9)
Those who cannot see the changes or refuse to think (8)
Those who see the changes in the long line of life (9)
Travis's present to Mama (3)
Walter though his wife should wear some ______ in this world. (6)
Walter's mother (4)
Walter's sister (8)
Walter's son (6)
Walter's wife (4)
What Beneatha wanted to study to be (6)
What Walter did on his day(s) away from work (5)
_______ Park (9)

A Raisin in the Sun Word Search 1 Answer Key

Words are placed backwards, forward, diagonally, up and down. Clues listed below can help you find the words. Circle the hidden vocabulary words in the maze.

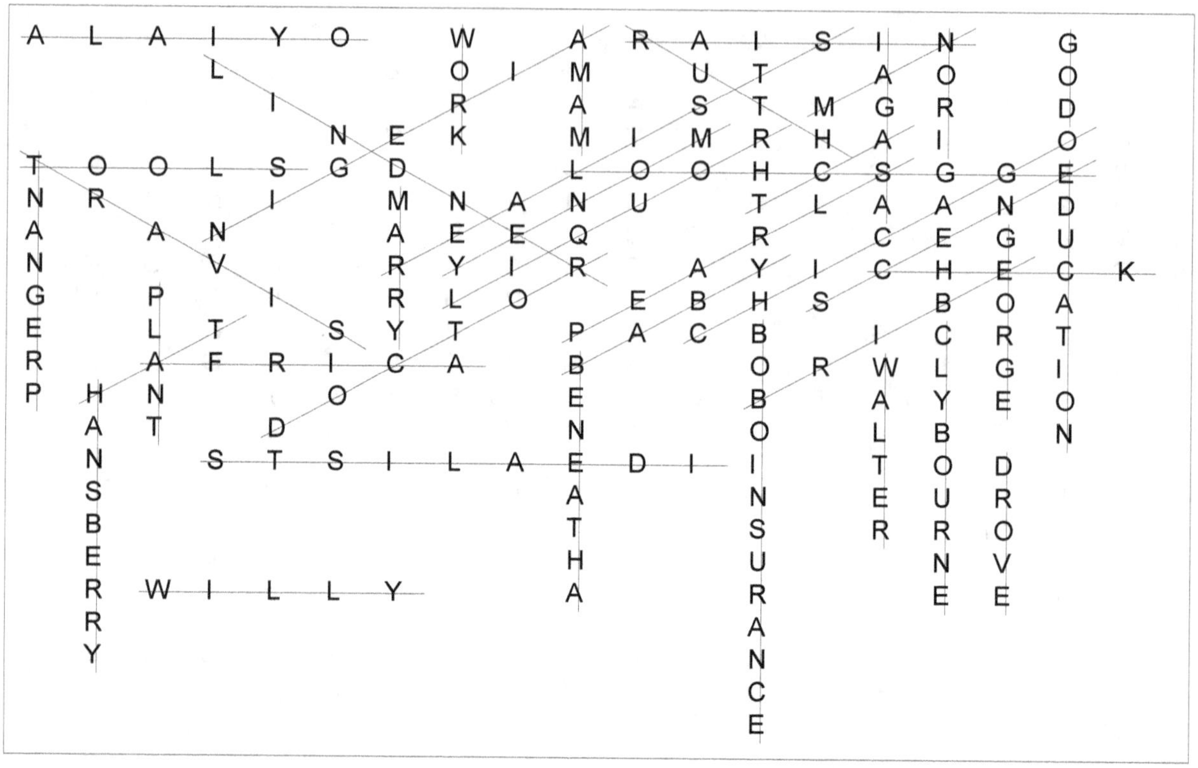

A __________ in the Sun (6)
Act division (5)
Asagai asked Beneatha to _______ him. (5)
Asagai's home continent (6)
Asagai's home county (7)
Author (9)
Beneatha did not believe in Him (3)
Beneatha wouldn't marry him because he was shallow (6)
Beneatha's African intellectual boyfriend (6)
City where Walter and Ruth live (7)
Daily job (4)
Damn all the _______ that ever was! (4)
Dollars (5)
Financial document made payable to Mama (5)
He brought Walter bad news about the money (4)
He ran off with the liquor store money (5)
He wanted to get more from life for himself and his family (6)
I tell you I am a __________!! (3)
Kind of store Walter wants to buy (6)
Last thing Mama takes from the apartment (5)
Mama got garden __________. (5)
Mama wanted to set money aside for Beneatha's (6)

One For Whom Bread-Food-Is Not Enough (6)
Pay-off; illegal money (5)
Play division (3)
Representative from the Clybourne Park Improvement Assoc. (7)
Ruth did it to the clothes (4)
Ruth was going to have one (4)
Ruth's with child condition (8)
Schooling (9)
Source of Mama's money (9)
Those who cannot see the changes or refuse to think (8)
Those who see the changes in the long line of life (9)
Travis's present to Mama (3)
Walter though his wife should wear some ______ in this world. (6)
Walter's mother (4)
Walter's sister (8)
Walter's son (6)
Walter's wife (4)
What Beneatha wanted to study to be (6)
What Walter did on his day(s) away from work (5)
_______ Park (9)

A Raisin in the Sun Word Search 2

Words are placed backwards, forward, diagonally, up and down. Clues listed below can help you find the words. Circle the hidden vocabulary words in the maze.

C	H	I	C	A	G	O	J	E	D	U	C	A	T	I	O	N	J	V
D	W	F	P	V	F	B	F	C	G	C	R	G	N	C	Y	M	G	V
G	V	L	R	C	K	N	V	V	T	Z	I	S	H	N	Q	M	F	F
Y	R	R	E	B	S	N	A	H	G	D	U	Q	V	W	K	H	V	R
M	P	S	G	Z	T	V	B	X	E	R	B	Y	Z	W	T	M	K	Y
Q	P	R	N	S	E	X	P	A	A	C	E	Q	D	S	L	K	T	T
N	L	O	A	P	G	Y	L	N	A	V	N	M	M	N	V	F	T	V
W	K	T	N	I	G	I	C	W	H	L	E	A	K	A	B	T	N	G
A	A	C	T	P	S	E	A	S	A	G	A	I	F	M	G	O	D	Y
L	N	O	B	T	N	I	T	W	T	I	T	I	A	R	R	R	B	Z
T	B	D	S	E	N	S	N	S	R	F	H	M	Y	I	I	G	Z	O
E	B	A	C	E	I	Z	B	E	P	P	A	W	N	O	R	C	Y	J
R	Y	S	B	L	C	S	G	C	L	K	L	E	Z	X	U	M	A	Q
B	D	I	A	Y	Y	I	W	E	R	I	N	A	Z	R	T	A	W	Y
J	R	E	R	Z	N	V	S	J	O	R	N	V	N	N	H	R	O	K
B	R	M	T	V	P	A	P	G	U	R	F	D	L	T	N	R	R	K
H	G	C	O	Y	Z	R	K	O	Q	W	G	S	N	C	P	Y	K	N
G	G	H	Y	N	H	T	B	C	I	S	D	E	C	E	X	J	F	C
F	S	E	S	J	E	Y	V	L	L	S	B	R	A	H	R	J	P	G
Q	F	C	V	W	L	Y	L	O	S	M	G	R	O	M	O	R	H	K
N	N	K	X	C	X	Y	O	H	K	W	L	D	W	V	V	O	Q	K
H	L	K	T	Q	T	T	G	F	H	S	Z	C	D	M	E	M	L	R

A __________ in the Sun (6)
Act division (5)
Asagai asked Beneatha to _______ him. (5)
Asagai's home continent (6)
Asagai's home county (7)
Author (9)
Beneatha did not believe in Him (3)
Beneatha wouldn't marry him because he was shallow (6)
Beneatha's African intellectual boyfriend (6)
City where Walter and Ruth live (7)
Daily job (4)
Damn all the _______ that ever was! (4)
Dollars (5)
Financial document made payable to Mama (5)
He brought Walter bad news about the money (4)
He ran off with the liquor store money (5)
He wanted to get more from life for himself and his family (6)
I tell you I am a __________!! (3)
Kind of store Walter wants to buy (6)
Last thing Mama takes from the apartment (5)
Mama got garden __________. (5)
Mama wanted to set money aside for Beneatha's (6)
One For Whom Bread-Food-Is Not Enough (6)
Pay-off; illegal money (5)
Play division (3)
Representative from the Clybourne Park Improvement Assoc. (7)
Ruth did it to the clothes (4)
Ruth was going to have one (4)
Ruth's with child condition (8)
Schooling (9)
Source of Mama's money (9)
Those who cannot see the changes or refuse to think (8)
Those who see the changes in the long line of life (9)
Travis's present to Mama (3)
Walter though his wife should wear some _______ in this world. (6)
Walter's mother (4)
Walter's sister (8)
Walter's son (6)
Walter's wife (4)
What Beneatha wanted to study to be (6)
What Walter did on his day(s) away from work (5)
_______ Park (9)

A Raisin in the Sun Word Search 2 Answer Key

Words are placed backwards, forward, diagonally, up and down. Clues listed below can help you find the words. Circle the hidden vocabulary words in the maze.

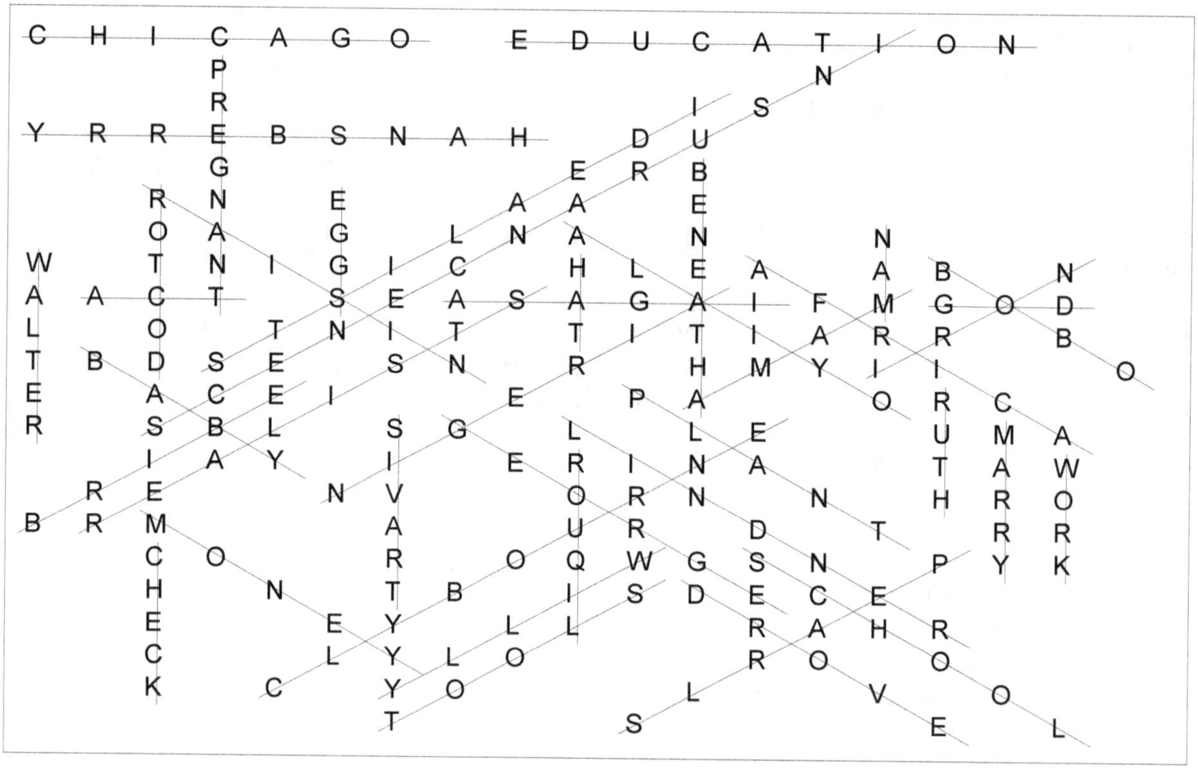

A __________ in the Sun (6)
Act division (5)
Asagai asked Beneatha to _______ him. (5)
Asagai's home continent (6)
Asagai's home county (7)
Author (9)
Beneatha did not believe in Him (3)
Beneatha wouldn't marry him because he was shallow (6)
Beneatha's African intellectual boyfriend (6)
City where Walter and Ruth live (7)
Daily job (4)
Damn all the _______ that ever was! (4)
Dollars (5)
Financial document made payable to Mama (5)
He brought Walter bad news about the money (4)
He ran off with the liquor store money (5)
He wanted to get more from life for himself and his family (6)
I tell you I am a __________!! (3)
Kind of store Walter wants to buy (6)
Last thing Mama takes from the apartment (5)
Mama got garden __________. (5)
Mama wanted to set money aside for Beneatha's (6)

One For Whom Bread-Food-Is Not Enough (6)
Pay-off; illegal money (5)
Play division (3)
Representative from the Clybourne Park Improvement Assoc. (7)
Ruth did it to the clothes (4)
Ruth was going to have one (4)
Ruth's with child condition (8)
Schooling (9)
Source of Mama's money (9)
Those who cannot see the changes or refuse to think (8)
Those who see the changes in the long line of life (9)
Travis's present to Mama (3)
Walter though his wife should wear some ______ in this world. (6)
Walter's mother (4)
Walter's sister (8)
Walter's son (6)
Walter's wife (4)
What Beneatha wanted to study to be (6)
What Walter did on his day(s) away from work (5)
_______ Park (9)

A Raisin in the Sun Word Search 3

Words are placed backwards, forward, diagonally, up and down. Words listed below are included in the maze. Circle the hidden vocabulary words in the maze.

L	I	N	D	N	E	R	D	G	J	Y	M	T	F	Q	P	T	P	N
N	O	I	T	A	C	U	D	E	E	F	G	G	K	S	L	X	V	Q
A	H	G	L	L	B	C	F	V	T	O	Y	K	W	V	A	T	C	K
Q	F	E	R	O	Y	L	I	Q	U	O	R	X	F	K	N	N	C	B
T	J	R	Z	O	M	R	Y	R	K	O	A	G	W	T	T	A	H	Z
G	S	I	I	H	A	H	Q	V	W	Q	I	Q	E	Z	S	N	E	T
B	O	A	N	C	M	X	S	N	I	B	S	S	E	W	I	G	C	B
B	A	D	A	S	A	G	A	I	D	F	I	S	C	E	N	E	K	Z
T	R	B	T	M	G	Z	C	O	E	V	N	L	N	S	O	R	P	X
M	A	I	Y	E	M	Y	C	C	A	F	M	O	A	L	I	P	B	G
M	L	H	B	H	A	T	R	R	L	W	S	O	R	R	T	B	D	H
Z	A	T	J	E	O	Y	T	C	I	T	G	T	U	A	A	E	D	H
G	I	R	D	R	L	K	L	G	S	P	H	T	S	E	L	N	S	T
M	Y	Z	R	L	B	F	K	I	T	I	H	P	N	P	I	E	R	D
P	O	K	I	Y	R	Q	L	X	S	A	R	Y	I	N	M	A	C	T
Z	B	W	R	E	B	A	F	Y	N	E	E	O	A	V	I	T	Z	F
D	O	M	V	Q	E	H	F	S	T	N	Z	M	N	X	S	H	X	F
H	B	O	G	R	J	Y	B	L	O	P	R	N	H	C	S	A	X	C
S	R	J	S	P	G	E	A	M	Q	V	V	F	X	Q	A	J	C	B
D	C	D	R	C	R	W	H	Y	K	X	R	M	P	S	F	N	H	K
R	C	E	N	R	U	O	B	Y	L	C	G	W	X	F	C	N	T	H
M	B	Z	Y	C	H	I	C	A	G	O	K	V	N	S	G	J	D	G

ACT	CLYBOURNE	IRON	RAISIN
AFRICA	DOCTOR	LINDNER	REALISTS
ALAIYO	DROVE	LIQUOR	RUTH
ASAGAI	EDUCATION	MAMA	SCENE
ASSIMILATIONIST	EGGS	MAN	SCHOOL
BABY	GEORGE	MARRY	TOOLS
BENEATHA	GOD	MONEY	TRAVIS
BOBO	HANSBERRY	NIGERIA	WALTER
BRIBE	HAT	PEARLS	WILLY
CHECK	IDEALISTS	PLANT	WORK
CHICAGO	INSURANCE	PREGNANT	

A Raisin in the Sun Word Search 3 Answer Key

Words are placed backwards, forward, diagonally, up and down. Words listed below are included in the maze. Circle the hidden vocabulary words in the maze.

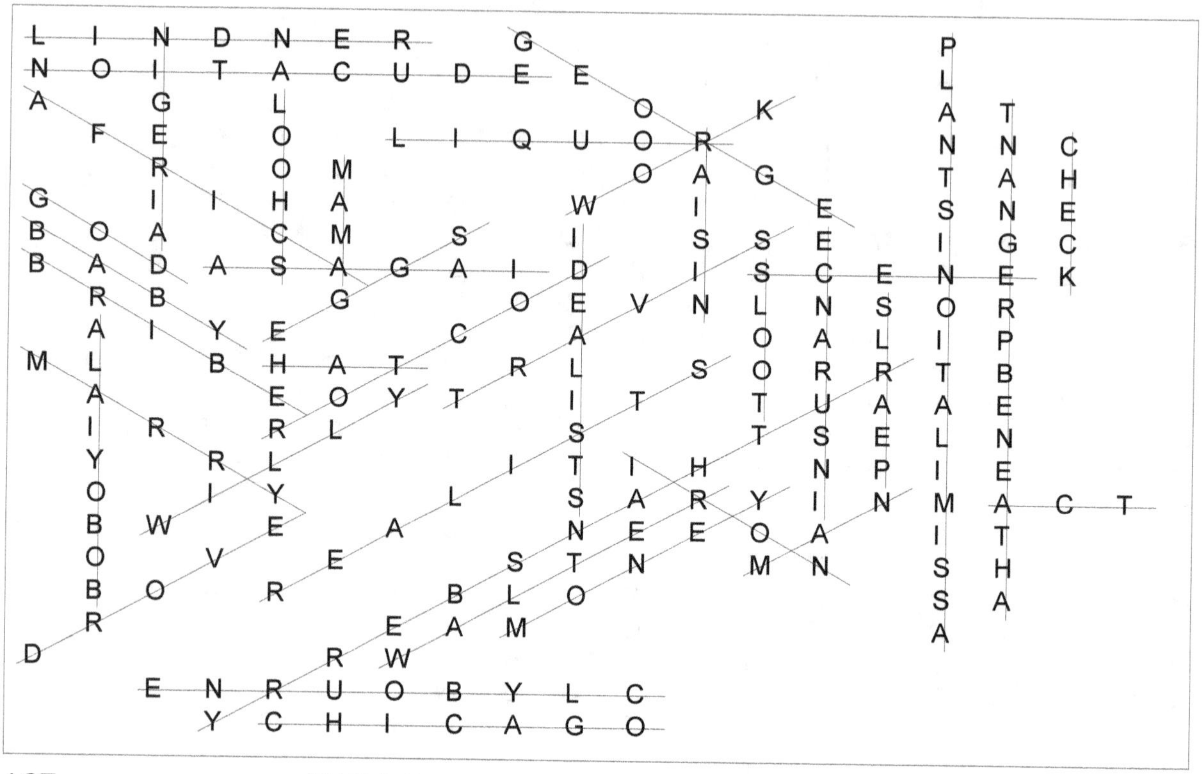

ACT	CLYBOURNE	IRON	RAISIN
AFRICA	DOCTOR	LINDNER	REALISTS
ALAIYO	DROVE	LIQUOR	RUTH
ASAGAI	EDUCATION	MAMA	SCENE
ASSIMILATIONIST	EGGS	MAN	SCHOOL
BABY	GEORGE	MARRY	TOOLS
BENEATHA	GOD	MONEY	TRAVIS
BOBO	HANSBERRY	NIGERIA	WALTER
BRIBE	HAT	PEARLS	WILLY
CHECK	IDEALISTS	PLANT	WORK
CHICAGO	INSURANCE	PREGNANT	

A Raisin in the Sun Word Search 4

Words are placed backwards, forward, diagonally, up and down. Words listed below are included in the maze. Circle the hidden vocabulary words in the maze.

S	X	I	N	I	G	E	R	I	A	T	S	J	A	L	K	Z	J	D
G	C	R	N	K	N	S	T	X	F	R	D	J	F	C	W	S	K	J
X	J	E	Q	S	X	K	M	M	M	A	T	V	R	H	F	P	V	L
R	H	Z	N	M	U	D	A	D	S	V	R	Y	I	E	K	L	S	Z
M	A	T	H	E	S	R	M	M	X	I	D	T	C	C	R	N	T	S
F	S	I	A	G	A	S	A	Z	P	S	T	R	A	K	O	H	S	P
H	N	R	S	R	R	R	J	N	L	H	C	B	J	Y	W	G	I	T
A	X	U	M	I	R	S	N	O	C	Q	K	H	I	R	G	M	L	S
T	W	T	G	Y	N	G	O	D	E	E	N	A	O	E	Z	W	A	I
Z	G	H	B	K	M	T	I	L	V	G	L	T	B	O	F	Q	E	N
S	L	A	F	X	O	B	T	I	O	A	C	H	O	Q	L	L	D	O
R	B	I	R	O	N	F	A	Q	R	O	J	A	B	X	B	E	I	I
D	R	G	N	C	E	Y	C	U	D	H	X	N	F	R	G	K	K	T
T	E	W	G	D	Y	C	U	O	P	P	H	S	I	R	B	Z	C	A
M	A	W	Y	V	N	N	D	R	R	C	G	B	O	Z	K	Y	L	L
P	L	A	N	T	G	E	E	P	E	O	E	E	W	I	L	L	Y	I
W	I	L	A	F	K	B	R	E	G	M	G	R	T	F	D	D	B	M
B	S	T	T	C	Z	J	C	A	N	F	V	R	N	B	P	T	O	I
C	T	E	P	Z	T	Z	C	R	A	F	V	Y	D	G	Z	V	U	S
D	S	R	C	T	D	I	Z	L	N	Y	V	P	H	N	J	V	R	S
P	Y	H	V	G	H	N	G	S	T	H	B	D	S	V	F	V	N	A
K	R	L	P	C	D	G	B	E	N	E	A	T	H	A	L	R	E	B

ACT
AFRICA
ALAIYO
ASAGAI
ASSIMILATIONIST
BABY
BENEATHA
BOBO
BRIBE
CHECK
CHICAGO
CLYBOURNE
DOCTOR
DROVE
EDUCATION
EGGS
GEORGE
GOD
HANSBERRY
HAT
IDEALISTS
INSURANCE
IRON
LINDNER
LIQUOR
MAMA
MAN
MARRY
MONEY
NIGERIA
PEARLS
PLANT
PREGNANT
RAISIN
REALISTS
RUTH
SCENE
SCHOOL
TOOLS
TRAVIS
WALTER
WILLY
WORK

A Raisin in the Sun Word Search 4 Answer Key

Words are placed backwards, forward, diagonally, up and down. Words listed below are included in the maze. Circle the hidden vocabulary words in the maze.

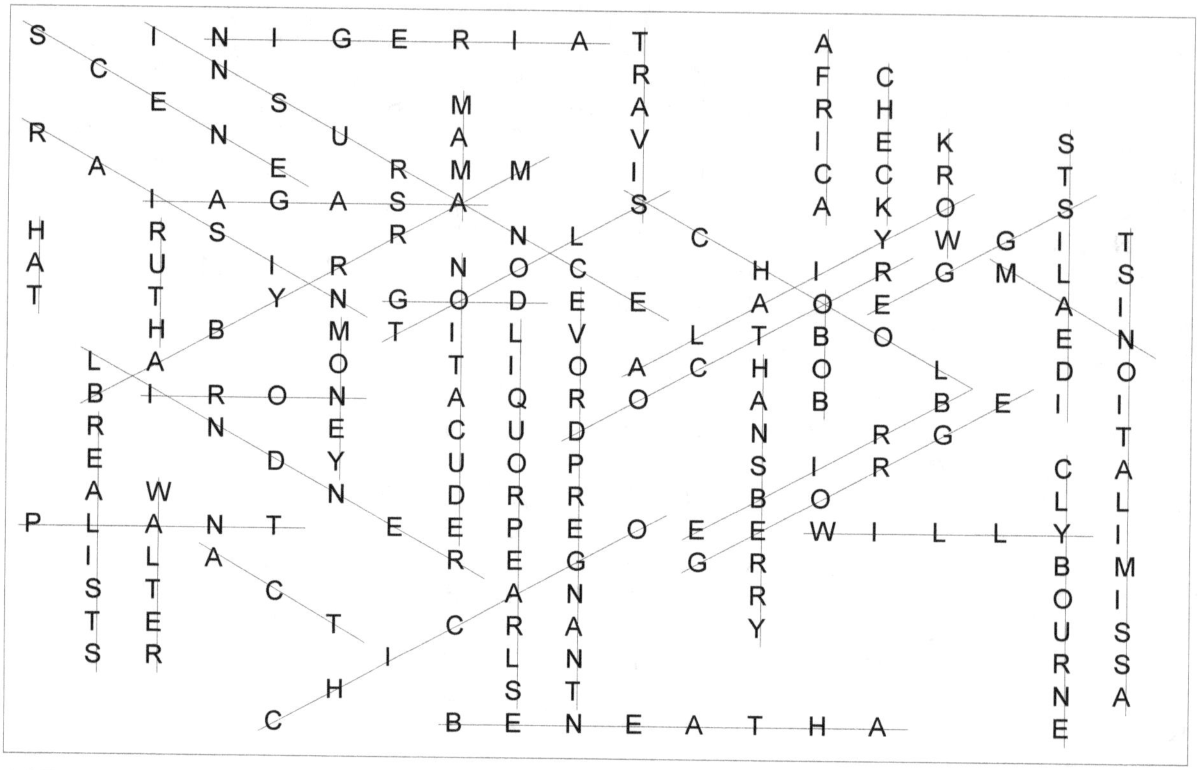

ACT	CLYBOURNE	IRON	RAISIN
AFRICA	DOCTOR	LINDNER	REALISTS
ALAIYO	DROVE	LIQUOR	RUTH
ASAGAI	EDUCATION	MAMA	SCENE
ASSIMILATIONIST	EGGS	MAN	SCHOOL
BABY	GEORGE	MARRY	TOOLS
BENEATHA	GOD	MONEY	TRAVIS
BOBO	HANSBERRY	NIGERIA	WALTER
BRIBE	HAT	PEARLS	WILLY
CHECK	IDEALISTS	PLANT	WORK
CHICAGO	INSURANCE	PREGNANT	

A Raisin in the Sun Crossword 1

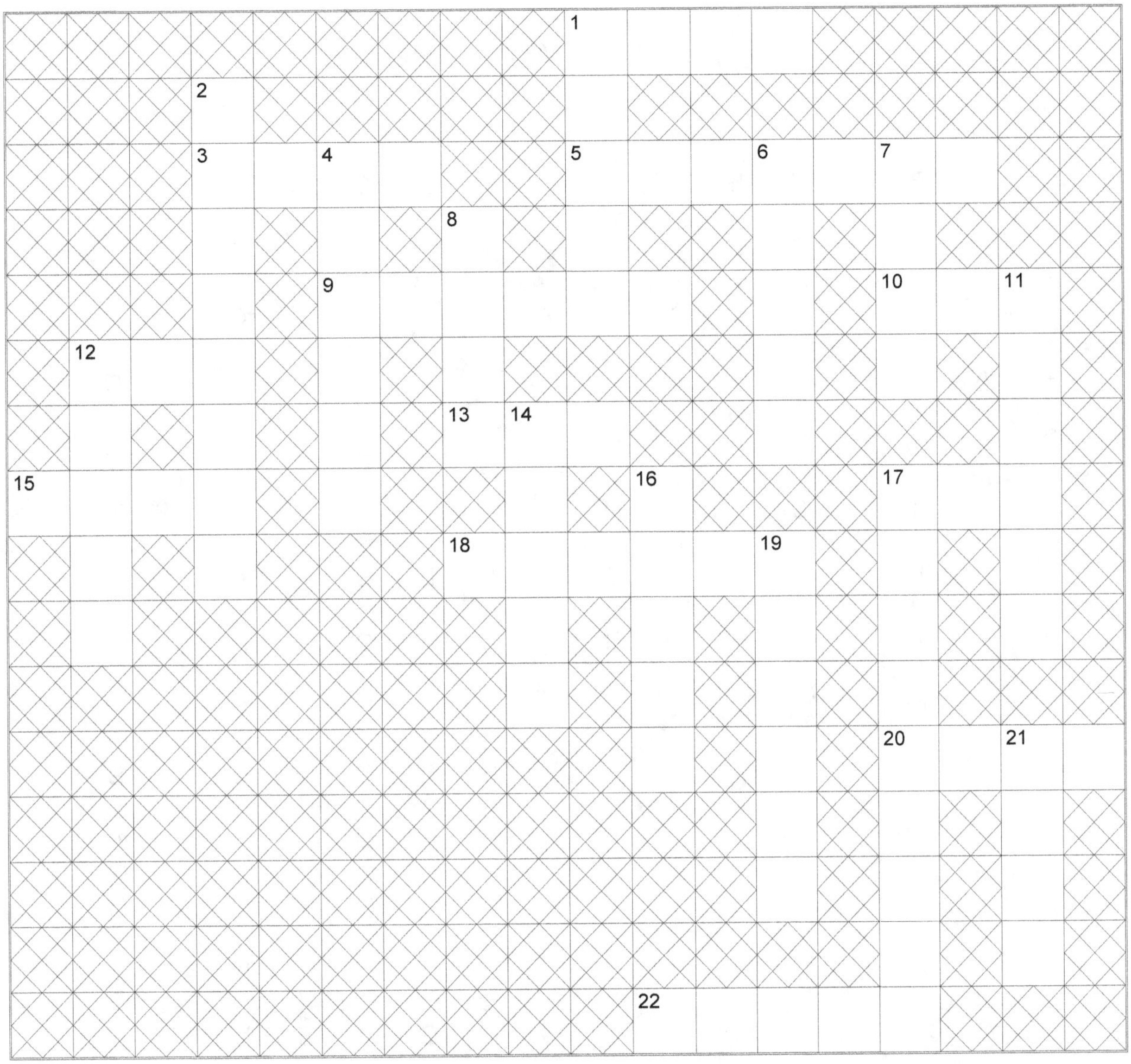

Across
1. Daily job
3. Walter's wife
5. Representative from the Clybourne Park Improvement Assoc.
9. One For Whom Bread-Food-Is Not Enough
10. Beneatha did not believe in Him
12. I tell you I am a __________!!
13. Play division
15. Ruth did it to the clothes
17. Travis's present to Mama
18. Walter though his wife should wear some ______ in this world.
20. He brought Walter bad news about the money
22. Dollars

.

Down
1. He ran off with the liquor store money
2. Ruth's with child condition
4. Walter's son
6. What Walter did on his day(s) away from work
7. Damn all the _______ that ever was!
8. Walter's mother
11. What Beneatha wanted to study to be
12. Asagai asked Beneatha to _______ him.
14. Financial document made payable to Mama
16. Pay-off; illegal money
17. Author
19. Mama wanted to set money aside for Beneatha's
21. Ruth was going to have one

A Raisin in the Sun Crossword 1 Answer Key

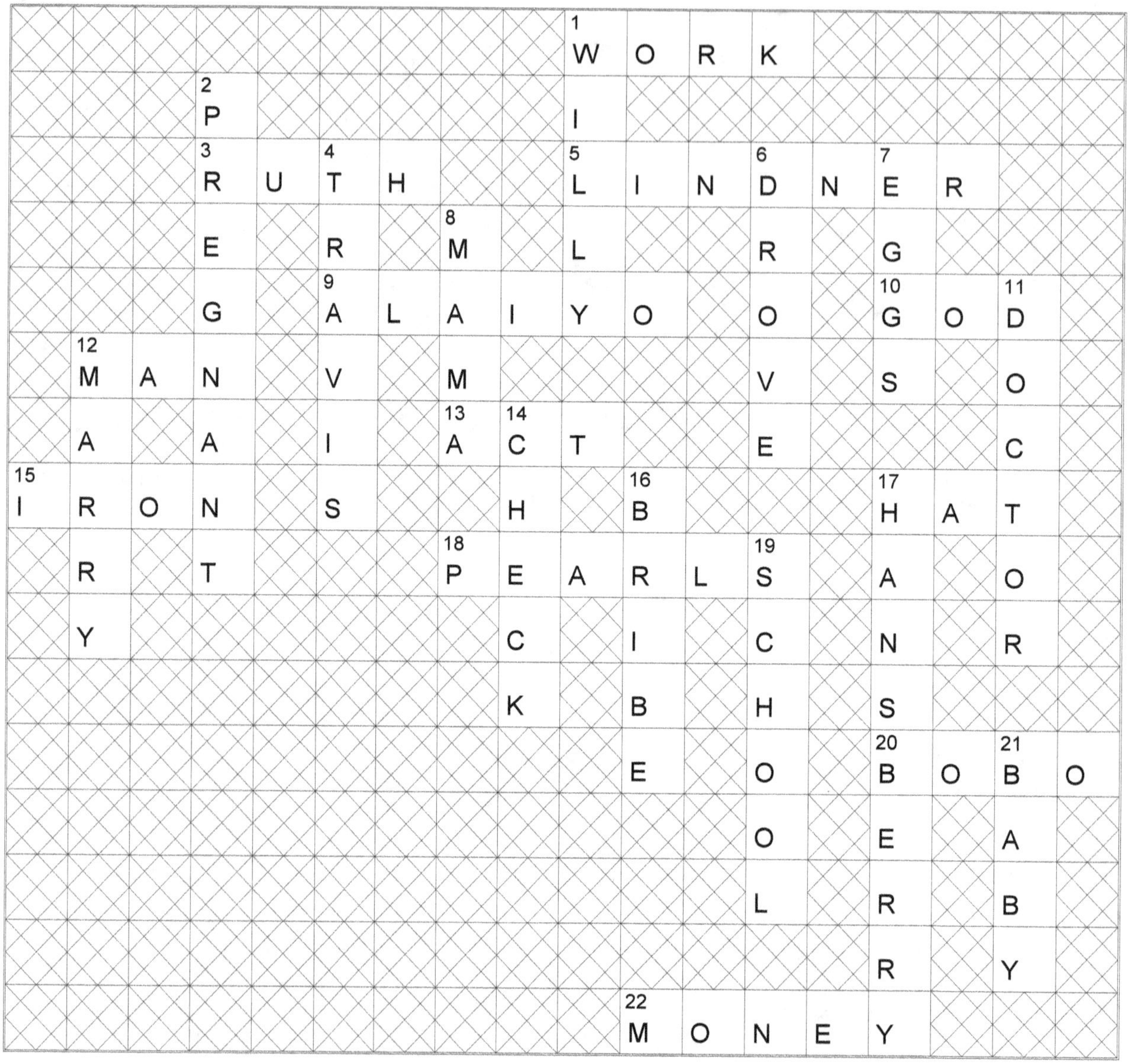

Across

1. Daily job
3. Walter's wife
5. Representative from the Clybourne Park Improvement Assoc.
9. One For Whom Bread-Food-Is Not Enough
10. Beneatha did not believe in Him
12. I tell you I am a ___________!!
13. Play division
15. Ruth did it to the clothes
17. Travis's present to Mama
18. Walter though his wife should wear some ______ in this world.
20. He brought Walter bad news about the money
22. Dollars

Down

1. He ran off with the liquor store money
2. Ruth's with child condition
4. Walter's son
6. What Walter did on his day(s) away from work
7. Damn all the ________ that ever was!
8. Walter's mother
11. What Beneatha wanted to study to be
12. Asagai asked Beneatha to ________ him.
14. Financial document made payable to Mama
16. Pay-off; illegal money
17. Author
19. Mama wanted to set money aside for Beneatha's
21. Ruth was going to have one

A Raisin in the Sun Crossword 2

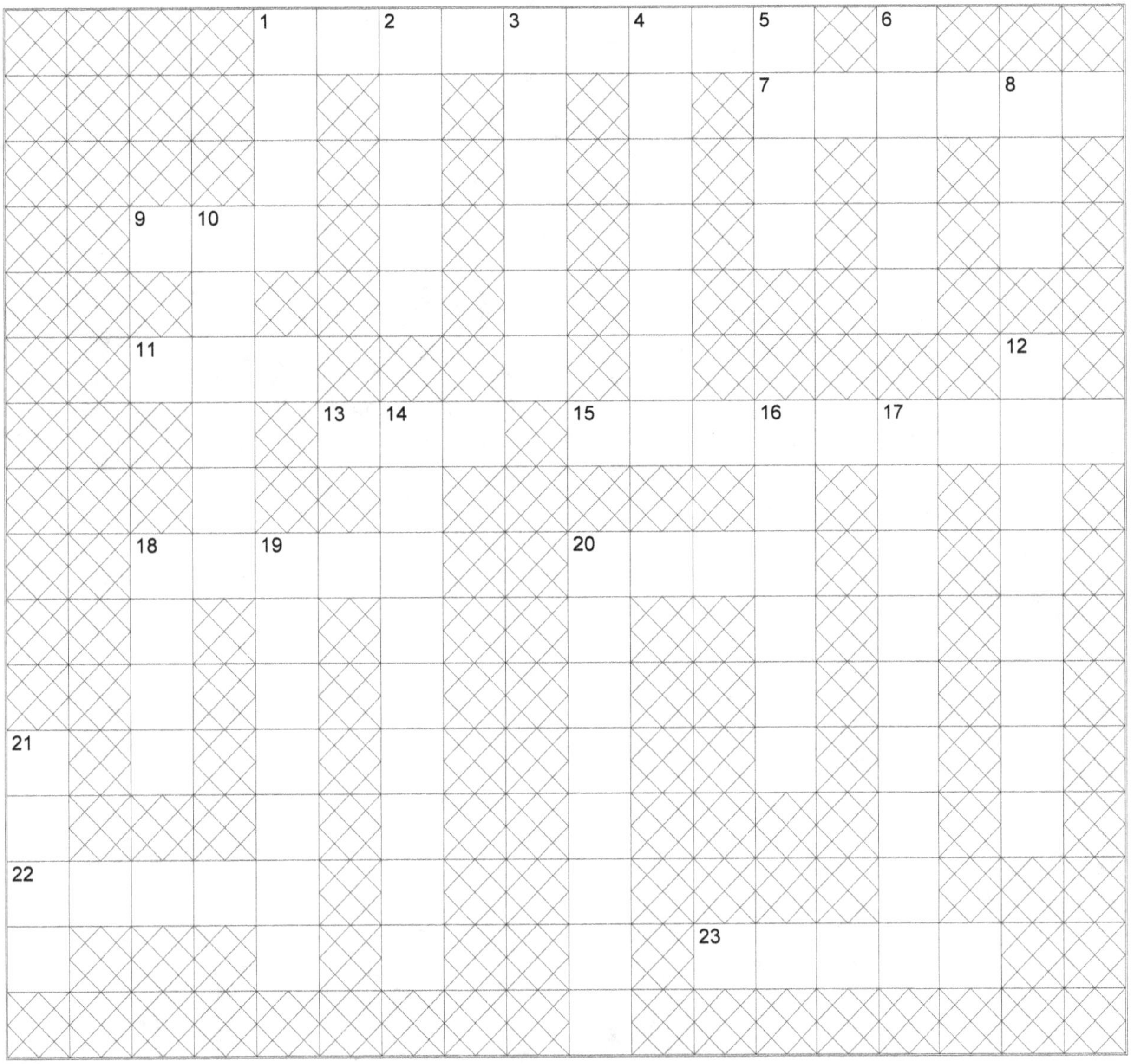

Across
1. Source of Mama's money
7. Beneatha wouldn't marry him because he was shallow
9. I tell you I am a __________!!
11. Travis's present to Mama
13. Play division
15. Author
18. He ran off with the liquor store money
20. Walter's wife
22. Pay-off; illegal money
23. Last thing Mama takes from the apartment

Down
1. Ruth did it to the clothes
2. Act division
3. A __________ in the Sun
4. Asagai's home county
5. Damn all the _______ that ever was!
6. Dollars
8. Beneatha did not believe in Him
10. Beneatha's African intellectual boyfriend
12. Ruth's with child condition
14. _______ Park
16. Mama wanted to set money aside for Beneatha's
17. Schooling
18. Daily job
19. Representative from the Clybourne Park Improvement Assoc.
20. Those who cannot see the changes or refuse to think
21. He brought Walter bad news about the money

A Raisin in the Sun Crossword 2 Answer Key

				1 I	N	2 S	U	3 R	A	4 N	C	5 E		6 M			
				R		C		A		I		7 G	E	O	R	8 G	E
				O		E		I		G		G		N		O	
		9 M	10 A	N		N		S		E		S		E		D	
			S			E		I		R				Y			
		11 H	A	T				N		I						12 P	
			G		13 A	14 C	T		15 H	A	N	16 S	B	17 E	R	R	Y
			A			L						C		D		E	
		18 W	I	19 L	L	Y			20 R	U	T	H		U		G	
		O		I		B			E			O		C		N	
		R		N		O			A			O		A		A	
21 B		K		D		U			L			L		T		N	
O				N		R			I					I		T	
22 B	R	I	B	E		N			S					O			
O				R		E			T		23 P	L	A	N	T		
									S								

Across
1. Source of Mama's money
7. Beneatha wouldn't marry him because he was shallow
9. I tell you I am a __________!!
11. Travis's present to Mama
13. Play division
15. Author
18. He ran off with the liquor store money
20. Walter's wife
22. Pay-off; illegal money
23. Last thing Mama takes from the apartment

Down
1. Ruth did it to the clothes
2. Act division
3. A __________ in the Sun
4. Asagai's home county
5. Damn all the _______ that ever was!
6. Dollars
8. Beneatha did not believe in Him
10. Beneatha's African intellectual boyfriend
12. Ruth's with child condition
14. _______ Park
16. Mama wanted to set money aside for Beneatha's
17. Schooling
18. Daily job
19. Representative from the Clybourne Park Improvement Assoc.
20. Those who cannot see the changes or refuse to think
21. He brought Walter bad news about the money

A Raisin in the Sun Crossword 3

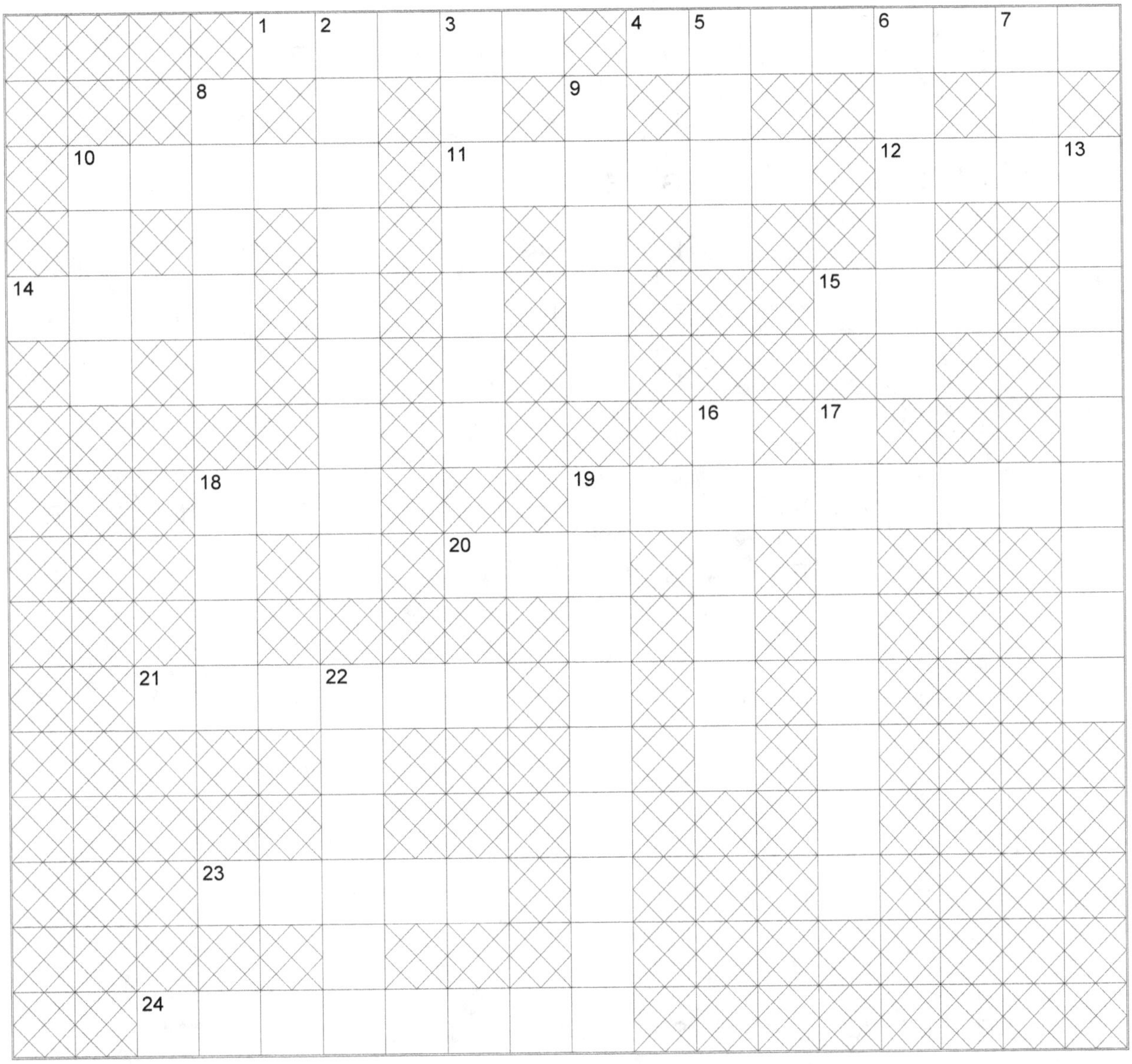

Across
1. Act division
4. Walter's sister
10. He ran off with the liquor store money
11. Beneatha wouldn't marry him because he was shallow
12. Walter's wife
14. Ruth did it to the clothes
15. Play division
18. I tell you I am a __________!!
19. Source of Mama's money
20. Beneatha did not believe in Him
21. A __________ in the Sun
23. Mama got garden __________.
24. Those who cannot see the changes or refuse to think

Down
2. _______ Park
3. Asagai's home county
5. Damn all the _______ that ever was!
6. Asagai's home continent
7. Travis's present to Mama
8. Last thing Mama takes from the apartment
9. Dollars
10. Daily job
13. Author
16. Beneatha's African intellectual boyfriend
17. Ruth's with child condition
18. Walter's mother
19. Those who see the changes in the long line of life
22. Mama wanted to set money aside for Beneatha's

A Raisin in the Sun Crossword 3 Answer Key

				1 S	2 C	E	3 N	E		4 B	5 E	N	E	6 A	T	7 H	A
			8 P		L		I		9 M		G			F		A	
	10 W	I	L	L	Y		11 G	E	O	R	G	E		12 R	U	T	13 H
	O		A		B		E		N		S			I			A
14 I	R	O	N		O		R		E				15 A	C	T		N
	K		T		U		I		Y					A			S
					R		A				16 A		17 P				B
			18 M	A	N				19 I	N	S	U	R	A	N	C	E
			A		E		20 G	O	D		A		E				R
			M						E		G		G				R
		21 R	A	I	22 S	I	N		A		A		N				Y
					C				L		I		A				
					H				I				N				
			23 T	O	O	L	S		S				T				
					O				T								
		24 R	E	A	L	I	S	T	S								

Across
1. Act division
4. Walter's sister
10. He ran off with the liquor store money
11. Beneatha wouldn't marry him because he was shallow
12. Walter's wife
14. Ruth did it to the clothes
15. Play division
18. I tell you I am a __________!!
19. Source of Mama's money
20. Beneatha did not believe in Him
21. A __________ in the Sun
23. Mama got garden __________.
24. Those who cannot see the changes or refuse to think

Down
2. _______ Park
3. Asagai's home county
5. Damn all the _______ that ever was!
6. Asagai's home continent
7. Travis's present to Mama
8. Last thing Mama takes from the apartment
9. Dollars
10. Daily job
13. Author
16. Beneatha's African intellectual boyfriend
17. Ruth's with child condition
18. Walter's mother
19. Those who see the changes in the long line of life
22. Mama wanted to set money aside for Beneatha's

A Raisin in the Sun Crossword 4

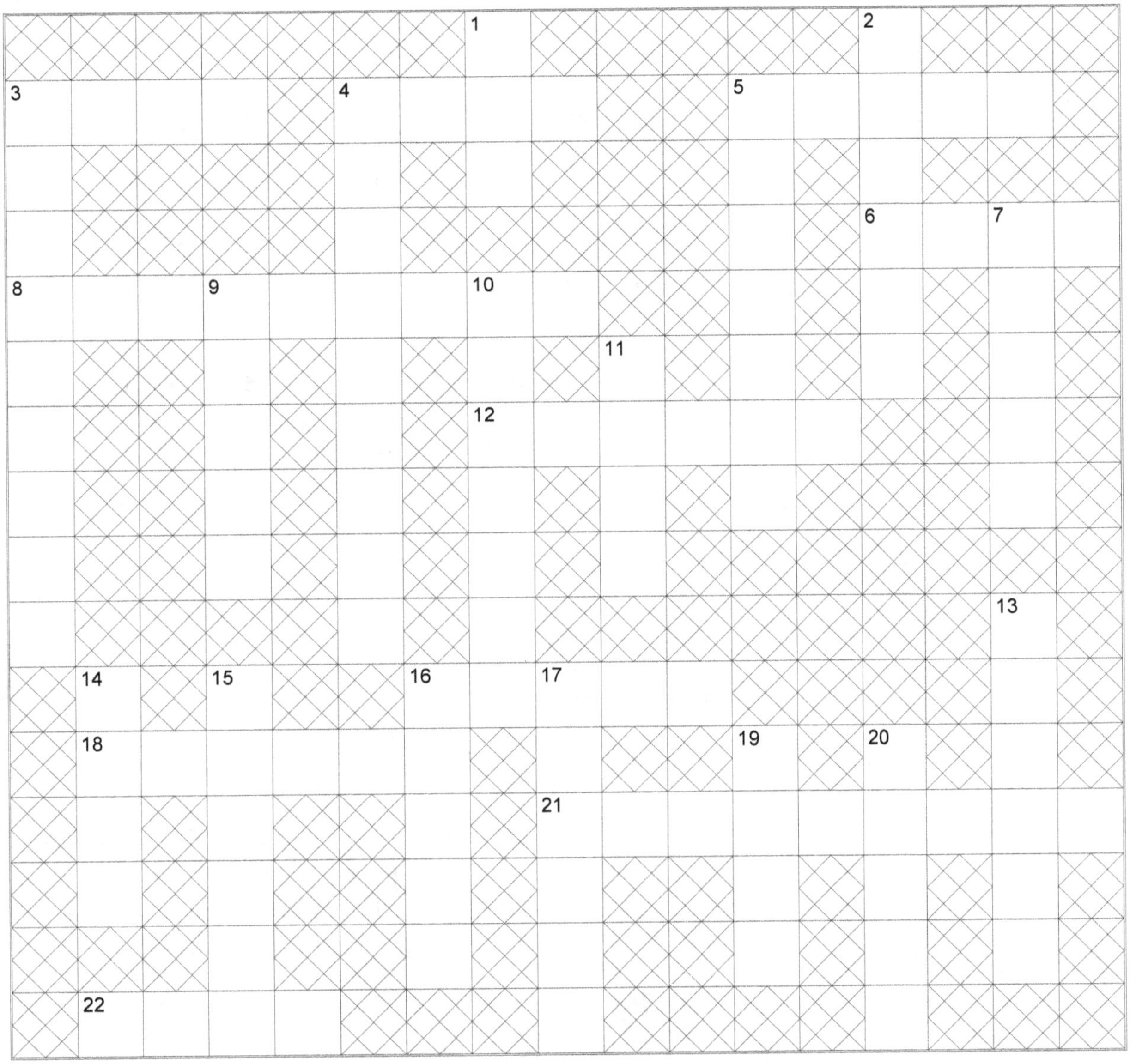

Across
3. Damn all the _______ that ever was!
4. Ruth did it to the clothes
5. Financial document made payable to Mama
6. Walter's wife
8. _______ Park
12. Beneatha wouldn't marry him because he was shallow
16. Asagai asked Beneatha to _______ him.
18. One For Whom Bread-Food-Is Not Enough
21. Those who see the changes in the long line of life
22. Daily job

Down
1. Beneatha did not believe in Him
2. Walter though his wife should wear some ______ in this world.
3. Schooling
4. Source of Mama's money
5. City where Walter and Ruth live
7. Mama got garden __________.
9. Pay-off; illegal money
10. Asagai's home county
11. He brought Walter bad news about the money
13. What Beneatha wanted to study to be
14. Ruth was going to have one
15. He wanted to get more from life for himself and his family
16. Dollars
17. A __________ in the Sun
19. Walter's mother
20. He ran off with the liquor store money

A Raisin in the Sun Crossword 4 Answer Key

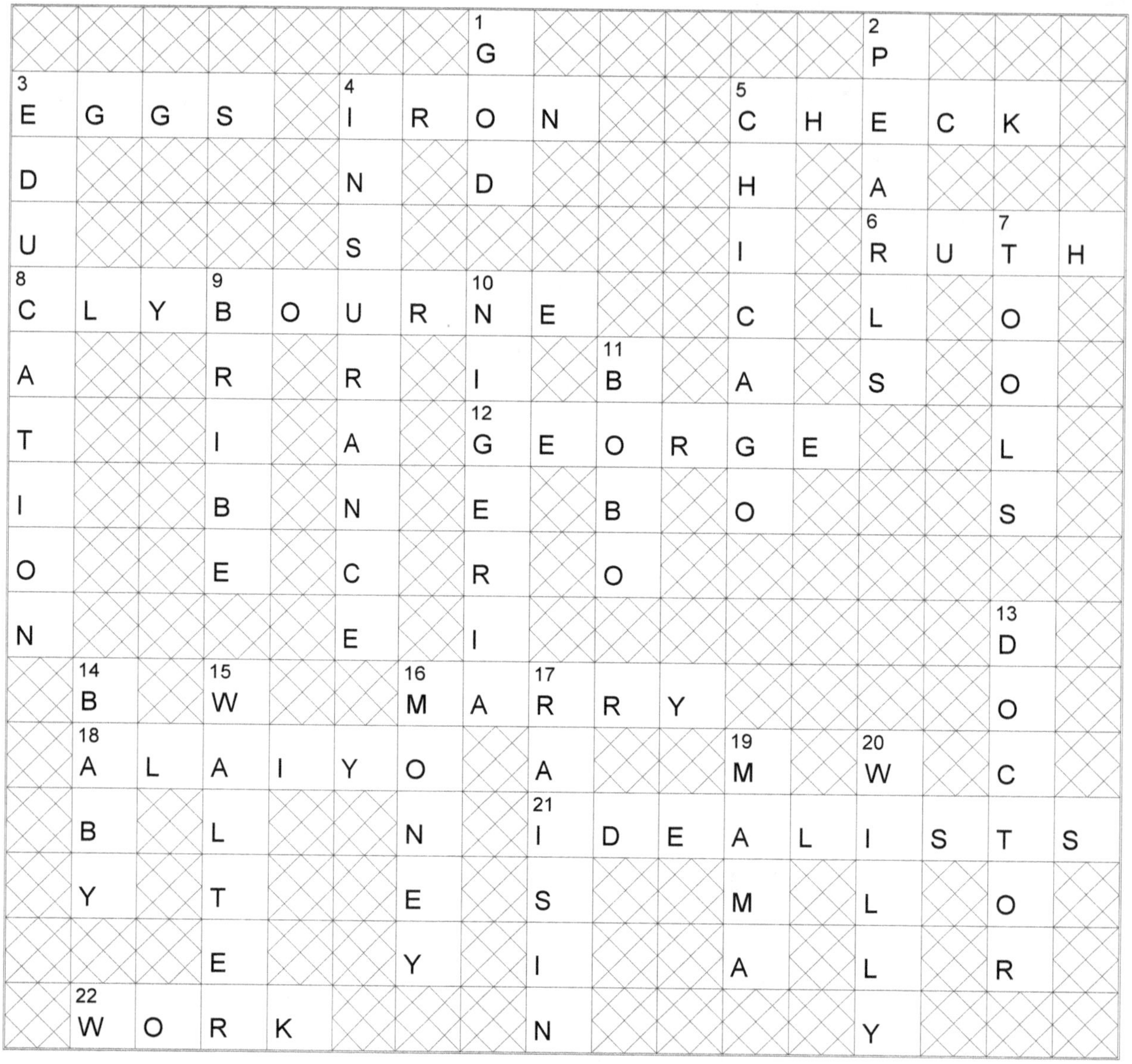

Across
3. Damn all the _______ that ever was!
4. Ruth did it to the clothes
5. Financial document made payable to Mama
6. Walter's wife
8. _______ Park
12. Beneatha wouldn't marry him because he was shallow
16. Asagai asked Beneatha to _______ him.
18. One For Whom Bread-Food-Is Not Enough
21. Those who see the changes in the long line of life
22. Daily job

Down
1. Beneatha did not believe in Him
2. Walter though his wife should wear some ______ in this world.
3. Schooling
4. Source of Mama's money
5. City where Walter and Ruth live
7. Mama got garden __________.
9. Pay-off; illegal money
10. Asagai's home county
11. He brought Walter bad news about the money
13. What Beneatha wanted to study to be
14. Ruth was going to have one
15. He wanted to get more from life for himself and his family
16. Dollars
17. A __________ in the Sun
19. Walter's mother
20. He ran off with the liquor store money

A Raisin in the Sun

NIGERIA	BENEATHA	IDEALISTS	MAN	MARRY
CHICAGO	BRIBE	TOOLS	DOCTOR	AFRICA
EGGS	EDUCATION	FREE SPACE	SCENE	CLYBOURNE
TRAVIS	REALISTS	GOD	PLANT	LIQUOR
RUTH	RAISIN	BABY	DROVE	HAT

A Raisin in the Sun

HANSBERRY	ASSIMILATIONIST	CHECK	GEORGE	SCHOOL
BOBO	INSURANCE	MONEY	ACT	WALTER
ALAIYO	PREGNANT	FREE SPACE	LINDNER	IRON
WILLY	ASAGAI	MAMA	HAT	DROVE
BABY	RAISIN	RUTH	LIQUOR	PLANT

A Raisin in the Sun

TRAVIS	MARRY	CHICAGO	HANSBERRY	PREGNANT
PLANT	GEORGE	DROVE	IDEALISTS	SCENE
ASSIMILATIONIST	BENEATHA	FREE SPACE	CLYBOURNE	RUTH
LIQUOR	MONEY	ASAGAI	INSURANCE	EDUCATION
ACT	SCHOOL	BABY	EGGS	RAISIN

A Raisin in the Sun

NIGERIA	CHECK	MAMA	MAN	AFRICA
BOBO	DOCTOR	GOD	IRON	ALAIYO
PEARLS	TOOLS	FREE SPACE	BRIBE	WILLY
WORK	LINDNER	HAT	RAISIN	EGGS
BABY	SCHOOL	ACT	EDUCATION	INSURANCE

A Raisin in the Sun

GEORGE	MARRY	IDEALISTS	MAMA	WALTER
TOOLS	SCENE	CLYBOURNE	ALAIYO	TRAVIS
CHICAGO	PLANT	FREE SPACE	GOD	DOCTOR
BOBO	AFRICA	REALISTS	PEARLS	HAT
MAN	MONEY	RUTH	EDUCATION	RAISIN

A Raisin in the Sun

BENEATHA	WORK	INSURANCE	BABY	ACT
ASAGAI	PREGNANT	BRIBE	WILLY	HANSBERRY
NIGERIA	LIQUOR	FREE SPACE	CHECK	EGGS
DROVE	SCHOOL	IRON	RAISIN	EDUCATION
RUTH	MONEY	MAN	HAT	PEARLS

A Raisin in the Sun

BRIBE	ASAGAI	CHICAGO	ASSIMILATIONIST	WILLY
BABY	DROVE	EGGS	HANSBERRY	REALISTS
CLYBOURNE	PLANT	FREE SPACE	MAN	RUTH
DOCTOR	CHECK	WORK	PEARLS	BENEATHA
RAISIN	LINDNER	EDUCATION	SCHOOL	MAMA

A Raisin in the Sun

GEORGE	LIQUOR	WALTER	TRAVIS	NIGERIA
ACT	BOBO	IDEALISTS	MONEY	SCENE
MARRY	INSURANCE	FREE SPACE	AFRICA	ALAIYO
TOOLS	IRON	PREGNANT	MAMA	SCHOOL
EDUCATION	LINDNER	RAISIN	BENEATHA	PEARLS

A Raisin in the Sun

BENEATHA	CHICAGO	DROVE	BRIBE	CLYBOURNE
EGGS	LINDNER	CHECK	RAISIN	GEORGE
INSURANCE	EDUCATION	FREE SPACE	MAMA	RUTH
MAN	HANSBERRY	WILLY	REALISTS	ALAIYO
WALTER	ASSIMILATIONIST	BABY	HAT	DOCTOR

A Raisin in the Sun

TOOLS	WORK	PREGNANT	SCENE	TRAVIS
NIGERIA	SCHOOL	PEARLS	LIQUOR	ACT
ASAGAI	GOD	FREE SPACE	MARRY	MONEY
IRON	AFRICA	IDEALISTS	DOCTOR	HAT
BABY	ASSIMILATIONIST	WALTER	ALAIYO	REALISTS

A Raisin in the Sun

WALTER	SCHOOL	BOBO	MAN	EDUCATION
TOOLS	PEARLS	WORK	ALAIYO	ACT
NIGERIA	DOCTOR	FREE SPACE	PREGNANT	DROVE
CHICAGO	GEORGE	CLYBOURNE	ASAGAI	HAT
IRON	RAISIN	BRIBE	IDEALISTS	BENEATHA

A Raisin in the Sun

MARRY	SCENE	TRAVIS	INSURANCE	BABY
EGGS	LIQUOR	HANSBERRY	LINDNER	AFRICA
MAMA	WILLY	FREE SPACE	GOD	PLANT
MONEY	REALISTS	RUTH	BENEATHA	IDEALISTS
BRIBE	RAISIN	IRON	HAT	ASAGAI

A Raisin in the Sun

BOBO	AFRICA	ACT	RAISIN	DROVE
BENEATHA	WILLY	IRON	SCENE	NIGERIA
MAN	EDUCATION	FREE SPACE	SCHOOL	WORK
MARRY	INSURANCE	IDEALISTS	EGGS	HANSBERRY
CHICAGO	CLYBOURNE	MAMA	ASSIMILATIONIST	MONEY

A Raisin in the Sun

PLANT	GOD	TOOLS	WALTER	CHECK
BABY	LIQUOR	PEARLS	ASAGAI	ALAIYO
DOCTOR	RUTH	FREE SPACE	BRIBE	HAT
GEORGE	PREGNANT	TRAVIS	MONEY	ASSIMILATIONIST
MAMA	CLYBOURNE	CHICAGO	HANSBERRY	EGGS

A Raisin in the Sun

BABY	IRON	CHECK	ALAIYO	SCENE
LINDNER	ACT	HANSBERRY	REALISTS	MARRY
SCHOOL	LIQUOR	FREE SPACE	EGGS	BOBO
DOCTOR	ASSIMILATIONIST	INSURANCE	BRIBE	WALTER
PLANT	HAT	MONEY	IDEALISTS	MAMA

A Raisin in the Sun

CLYBOURNE	PEARLS	BENEATHA	MAN	RUTH
NIGERIA	TOOLS	RAISIN	WILLY	GEORGE
EDUCATION	ASAGAI	FREE SPACE	GOD	AFRICA
DROVE	PREGNANT	TRAVIS	MAMA	IDEALISTS
MONEY	HAT	PLANT	WALTER	BRIBE

A Raisin in the Sun

HANSBERRY	WALTER	MAN	SCHOOL	LIQUOR
CLYBOURNE	DOCTOR	REALISTS	TOOLS	EDUCATION
ALAIYO	NIGERIA	FREE SPACE	BABY	WILLY
SCENE	WORK	CHICAGO	RUTH	LINDNER
RAISIN	ACT	BOBO	MONEY	DROVE

A Raisin in the Sun

IDEALISTS	IRON	AFRICA	MAMA	CHECK
PLANT	EGGS	BENEATHA	MARRY	GOD
TRAVIS	PEARLS	FREE SPACE	INSURANCE	BRIBE
ASAGAI	ASSIMILATIONIST	GEORGE	DROVE	MONEY
BOBO	ACT	RAISIN	LINDNER	RUTH

A Raisin in the Sun

TRAVIS	AFRICA	MAMA	CHICAGO	GEORGE
WORK	PLANT	INSURANCE	RUTH	TOOLS
GOD	ASAGAI	FREE SPACE	MARRY	ASSIMILATIONIST
HANSBERRY	EGGS	REALISTS	IDEALISTS	WALTER
ALAIYO	BOBO	EDUCATION	BENEATHA	WILLY

A Raisin in the Sun

CLYBOURNE	IRON	LINDNER	NIGERIA	RAISIN
SCHOOL	BRIBE	LIQUOR	MONEY	SCENE
PREGNANT	ACT	FREE SPACE	MAN	BABY
PEARLS	HAT	DOCTOR	WILLY	BENEATHA
EDUCATION	BOBO	ALAIYO	WALTER	IDEALISTS

A Raisin in the Sun

GOD	SCENE	RAISIN	TOOLS	INSURANCE
REALISTS	RUTH	LIQUOR	WALTER	EDUCATION
PREGNANT	CLYBOURNE	FREE SPACE	MARRY	MAMA
EGGS	CHICAGO	HANSBERRY	BABY	DROVE
MAN	ASAGAI	WORK	ALAIYO	BRIBE

A Raisin in the Sun

ASSIMILATIONIST	SCHOOL	LINDNER	MONEY	IRON
BENEATHA	BOBO	ACT	GEORGE	PLANT
IDEALISTS	HAT	FREE SPACE	AFRICA	TRAVIS
DOCTOR	CHECK	WILLY	BRIBE	ALAIYO
WORK	ASAGAI	MAN	DROVE	BABY

A Raisin in the Sun

WILLY	CHECK	EGGS	AFRICA	ASAGAI
PREGNANT	GEORGE	LINDNER	PLANT	BRIBE
ALAIYO	MONEY	FREE SPACE	HANSBERRY	CHICAGO
REALISTS	MAN	IDEALISTS	INSURANCE	IRON
RAISIN	LIQUOR	DROVE	SCHOOL	BENEATHA

A Raisin in the Sun

NIGERIA	EDUCATION	ASSIMILATIONIST	ACT	TOOLS
GOD	PEARLS	DOCTOR	CLYBOURNE	RUTH
BABY	HAT	FREE SPACE	WORK	BOBO
TRAVIS	WALTER	MARRY	BENEATHA	SCHOOL
DROVE	LIQUOR	RAISIN	IRON	INSURANCE

A Raisin in the Sun

ACT	LINDNER	PREGNANT	EGGS	PEARLS
SCHOOL	CHICAGO	MARRY	HAT	MAMA
IDEALISTS	PLANT	FREE SPACE	DROVE	MONEY
AFRICA	TOOLS	CHECK	TRAVIS	BABY
ASAGAI	GEORGE	WORK	GOD	BENEATHA

A Raisin in the Sun

NIGERIA	RAISIN	SCENE	INSURANCE	ALAIYO
RUTH	IRON	WALTER	BOBO	REALISTS
MAN	BRIBE	FREE SPACE	WILLY	EDUCATION
LIQUOR	CLYBOURNE	DOCTOR	BENEATHA	GOD
WORK	GEORGE	ASAGAI	BABY	TRAVIS

A Raisin in the Sun

LINDNER	ASSIMILATIONIST	DOCTOR	BABY	MAN
RUTH	SCHOOL	BRIBE	ACT	NIGERIA
SCENE	CLYBOURNE	FREE SPACE	DROVE	WORK
WALTER	BENEATHA	TOOLS	HAT	INSURANCE
CHICAGO	BOBO	ALAIYO	GEORGE	MAMA

A Raisin in the Sun

AFRICA	CHECK	PREGNANT	MONEY	WILLY
IDEALISTS	PEARLS	MARRY	RAISIN	PLANT
ASAGAI	TRAVIS	FREE SPACE	HANSBERRY	IRON
GOD	LIQUOR	EGGS	MAMA	GEORGE
ALAIYO	BOBO	CHICAGO	INSURANCE	HAT

A Raisin in the Sun

EDUCATION	BABY	IDEALISTS	WORK	MARRY
SCENE	PREGNANT	BRIBE	GOD	ACT
ASAGAI	INSURANCE	FREE SPACE	PLANT	TOOLS
IRON	MAMA	LIQUOR	MONEY	SCHOOL
ALAIYO	BOBO	WILLY	MAN	DOCTOR

A Raisin in the Sun

ASSIMILATIONIST	DROVE	AFRICA	BENEATHA	HANSBERRY
REALISTS	EGGS	GEORGE	TRAVIS	LINDNER
RAISIN	HAT	FREE SPACE	RUTH	NIGERIA
PEARLS	CLYBOURNE	WALTER	DOCTOR	MAN
WILLY	BOBO	ALAIYO	SCHOOL	MONEY

A Raisin in the Sun

BOBO	BRIBE	PLANT	PREGNANT	DROVE
TRAVIS	LINDNER	MARRY	ACT	WILLY
ALAIYO	CHICAGO	FREE SPACE	CLYBOURNE	AFRICA
MAMA	TOOLS	SCHOOL	EGGS	HANSBERRY
LIQUOR	MONEY	INSURANCE	PEARLS	RAISIN

A Raisin in the Sun

HAT	NIGERIA	GEORGE	CHECK	EDUCATION
SCENE	REALISTS	RUTH	WALTER	WORK
GOD	IRON	FREE SPACE	ASSIMILATIONIST	IDEALISTS
BABY	DOCTOR	ASAGAI	RAISIN	PEARLS
INSURANCE	MONEY	LIQUOR	HANSBERRY	EGGS

A Raisin in the Sun Vocabulary Word List

No. Word	Clue/Definition
1. AMIABLY	Good naturedly
2. AMID	Among; in the midst of
3. ARROGANT	Overbearingly proud; haughty
4. ASSIMILATIONISM	Belief that minority cultures should dissolve into a dominant culture
5. CLICHE	Trite or overused expression or idea
6. COQUETTISHLY	In a manner befitting a woman who flirts with men
7. DESPAIR	Hopelessness
8. DESPERATION	Condition of being driven to take almost any risk as a last resort
9. ECCENTRIC	Deviating from the established norm, model or rule
10. EPITAPH	Inscription on a tombstone; summary of a deceased person's life
11. EXASPERATED	Irritated; provoked; irked
12. EXUBERANCE	Having unrestrained high spirtis; being overjoyed
13. FORLORNLY	Looking pitiful, desperate or hopeless
14. FURTIVELY	Stealthily; expressive of hidden motives
15. FUTILE	Useless
16. HAPHAZARDLY	Without care; characterized by chance
17. HEATHENISM	Religion of those who don't beleive in God and/or are uncivilized
18. INAPPROPRIATELY	Unsuitably; improperly
19. INSINUATINGLY	With more meaning than the spoken word; implying
20. LUDICROUS	Laughably ridiculous
21. MENACINGLY	Threateningly
22. MONOLOGUE	Long speech or talk made by one person
23. MUTILATED	Maimed; damaged
24. OMINOUS	Menacing; threatening
25. OPPRESSIVE	Tyrannical
26. PENETRATED	Pierced; affected; diffused
27. PLAINTIVELY	Sorrowfully
28. PLUNDER	To rob of goods by force; loot
29. PRESUMABLY	Probably; reasonably supposed
30. PROPOSITION	Suggested plan
31. REBUFFS	Bluntly refuses
32. REVELATION	Some new information; news
33. SARCASTICALLY	In a manner using statements or implications opposite to the underlying meaning
34. TENTATIVELY	Uncertainly
35. TYRANT	Ruler who exercises power in a harsh, cruel manner
36. UNDISTINGUISHED	Common; nothing special
37. VENGEANCE	With violence or fury
38. VICIOUSLY	Violently; maliciously
39. VINDICATED	Cleared of accusations, blame or suspicion
40. WROUGHT	Shaped; made

A Raisin in the Sun Vocabulary Fill In The Blanks 1

1. Cleared of accusations, blame or suspicion
2. Irritated; provoked; irked
3. Ruler who exercises power in a harsh, cruel manner
4. Trite or overused expression or idea
5. Threateningly
6. Overbearingly proud; haughty
7. Without care; characterized by chance
8. Stealthily; expressive of hidden motives
9. In a manner befitting a woman who flirts with men
10. Useless
11. Sorrowfully
12. Religion of those who don't beleive in God and/or are uncivilized
13. Inscription on a tombstone; summary of a deceased person's life
14. Some new information; news
15. In a manner using statements or implications opposite to the underlying meaning
16. Tyrannical
17. Pierced; affected; diffused
18. Unsuitably; improperly
19. Long speech or talk made by one person
20. Common; nothing special

A Raisin in the Sun Vocabulary Fill In The Blanks 1 Answer Key

VINDICATED	1. Cleared of accusations, blame or suspicion
EXASPERATED	2. Irritated; provoked; irked
TYRANT	3. Ruler who exercises power in a harsh, cruel manner
CLICHE	4. Trite or overused expression or idea
MENACINGLY	5. Threateningly
ARROGANT	6. Overbearingly proud; haughty
HAPHAZARDLY	7. Without care; characterized by chance
FURTIVELY	8. Stealthily; expressive of hidden motives
COQUETTISHLY	9. In a manner befitting a woman who flirts with men
FUTILE	10. Useless
PLAINTIVELY	11. Sorrowfully
HEATHENISM	12. Religion of those who don't beleive in God and/or are uncivilized
EPITAPH	13. Inscription on a tombstone; summary of a deceased person's life
REVELATION	14. Some new information; news
SARCASTICALLY	15. In a manner using statements or implications opposite to the underlying meaning
OPPRESSIVE	16. Tyrannical
PENETRATED	17. Pierced; affected; diffused
INAPPROPRIATELY	18. Unsuitably; improperly
MONOLOGUE	19. Long speech or talk made by one person
UNDISTINGUISHED	20. Common; nothing special

A Raisin in the Sun Vocabulary Fill In The Blanks 2

1. Inscription on a tombstone; summary of a deceased person's life
2. Ruler who exercises power in a harsh, cruel manner
3. Deviating from the established norm, model or rule
4. With more meaning than the spoken word; implying
5. Unsuitably; improperly
6. Looking pitiful, desperate or hopeless
7. Religion of those who don't beleive in God and/or are uncivilized
8. Probably; reasonably supposed
9. Laughably ridiculous
10. Sorrowfully
11. Overbearingly proud; haughty
12. Tyrannical
13. Trite or overused expression or idea
14. Suggested plan
15. Belief that minority cultures should dissolve into a dominant culture
16. Menacing; threatening
17. Some new information; news
18. Without care; characterized by chance
19. Bluntly refuses
20. With violence or fury

A Raisin in the Sun Vocabulary Fill In The Blanks 2 Answer Key

EPITAPH	1. Inscription on a tombstone; summary of a deceased person's life
TYRANT	2. Ruler who exercises power in a harsh, cruel manner
ECCENTRIC	3. Deviating from the established norm, model or rule
INSINUATINGLY	4. With more meaning than the spoken word; implying
INAPPROPRIATELY	5. Unsuitably; improperly
FORLORNLY	6. Looking pitiful, desperate or hopeless
HEATHENISM	7. Religion of those who don't beleive in God and/or are uncivilized
PRESUMABLY	8. Probably; reasonably supposed
LUDICROUS	9. Laughably ridiculous
PLAINTIVELY	10. Sorrowfully
ARROGANT	11. Overbearingly proud; haughty
OPPRESSIVE	12. Tyrannical
CLICHE	13. Trite or overused expression or idea
PROPOSITION	14. Suggested plan
ASSIMILATIONISM	15. Belief that minority cultures should dissolve into a dominant culture
OMINOUS	16. Menacing; threatening
REVELATION	17. Some new information; news
HAPHAZARDLY	18. Without care; characterized by chance
REBUFFS	19. Bluntly refuses
VENGEANCE	20. With violence or fury

A Raisin in the Sun Vocabulary Fill In The Blanks 3

_______________ 1. Unsuitably; improperly

_______________ 2. Belief that minority cultures should dissolve into a dominant culture

_______________ 3. Good naturedly

_______________ 4. Overbearingly proud; haughty

_______________ 5. Shaped; made

_______________ 6. Laughably ridiculous

_______________ 7. Deviating from the established norm, model or rule

_______________ 8. Bluntly refuses

_______________ 9. Without care; characterized by chance

_______________ 10. Suggested plan

_______________ 11. Looking pitiful, desperate or hopeless

_______________ 12. In a manner using statements or implications opposite to the underlying meaning

_______________ 13. Trite or overused expression or idea

_______________ 14. Useless

_______________ 15. Long speech or talk made by one person

_______________ 16. Religion of those who don't beleive in God and/or are uncivilized

_______________ 17. Ruler who exercises power in a harsh, cruel manner

_______________ 18. Sorrowfully

_______________ 19. Having unrestrained high spirtis; being overjoyed

_______________ 20. Common; nothing special

A Raisin in the Sun Vocabulary Fill In The Blanks 3 Answer Key

INAPPROPRIATELY	1. Unsuitably; improperly
ASSIMILATIONISM	2. Belief that minority cultures should dissolve into a dominant culture
AMIABLY	3. Good naturedly
ARROGANT	4. Overbearingly proud; haughty
WROUGHT	5. Shaped; made
LUDICROUS	6. Laughably ridiculous
ECCENTRIC	7. Deviating from the established norm, model or rule
REBUFFS	8. Bluntly refuses
HAPHAZARDLY	9. Without care; characterized by chance
PROPOSITION	10. Suggested plan
FORLORNLY	11. Looking pitiful, desperate or hopeless
SARCASTICALLY	12. In a manner using statements or implications opposite to the underlying meaning
CLICHE	13. Trite or overused expression or idea
FUTILE	14. Useless
MONOLOGUE	15. Long speech or talk made by one person
HEATHENISM	16. Religion of those who don't beleive in God and/or are uncivilized
TYRANT	17. Ruler who exercises power in a harsh, cruel manner
PLAINTIVELY	18. Sorrowfully
EXUBERANCE	19. Having unrestrained high spirtis; being overjoyed
UNDISTINGUISHED	20. Common; nothing special

A Raisin in the Sun Vocabulary Fill In The Blanks 4

1. Good naturedly
2. Menacing; threatening
3. Among; in the midst of
4. Pierced; affected; diffused
5. Laughably ridiculous
6. Unsuitably; improperly
7. Uncertainly
8. Looking pitiful, desperate or hopeless
9. Common; nothing special
10. Suggested plan
11. Useless
12. Shaped; made
13. With more meaning than the spoken word; implying
14. Cleared of accusations, blame or suspicion
15. Without care; characterized by chance
16. Bluntly refuses
17. Probably; reasonably supposed
18. Sorrowfully
19. In a manner using statements or implications opposite to the underlying meaning
20. Overbearingly proud; haughty

A Raisin in the Sun Vocabulary Fill In The Blanks 4 Answer Key

AMIABLY	1. Good naturedly
OMINOUS	2. Menacing; threatening
AMID	3. Among; in the midst of
PENETRATED	4. Pierced; affected; diffused
LUDICROUS	5. Laughably ridiculous
INAPPROPRIATELY	6. Unsuitably; improperly
TENTATIVELY	7. Uncertainly
FORLORNLY	8. Looking pitiful, desperate or hopeless
UNDISTINGUISHED	9. Common; nothing special
PROPOSITION	10. Suggested plan
FUTILE	11. Useless
WROUGHT	12. Shaped; made
INSINUATINGLY	13. With more meaning than the spoken word; implying
VINDICATED	14. Cleared of accusations, blame or suspicion
HAPHAZARDLY	15. Without care; characterized by chance
REBUFFS	16. Bluntly refuses
PRESUMABLY	17. Probably; reasonably supposed
PLAINTIVELY	18. Sorrowfully
SARCASTICALLY	19. In a manner using statements or implications opposite to the underlying meaning
ARROGANT	20. Overbearingly proud; haughty

A Raisin in the Sun Vocabulary Matching 1

___ 1. SARCASTICALLY	A. Violently; maliciously
___ 2. AMID	B. Irritated; provoked; irked
___ 3. INSINUATINGLY	C. To rob of goods by force; loot
___ 4. PLAINTIVELY	D. Laughably ridiculous
___ 5. ARROGANT	E. Among; in the midst of
___ 6. HEATHENISM	F. Condition of being driven to take almost any risk as a last resort
___ 7. EXASPERATED	G. Bluntly refuses
___ 8. COQUETTISHLY	H. With more meaning than the spoken word; implying
___ 9. TENTATIVELY	I. Useless
___10. VICIOUSLY	J. Uncertainly
___11. PRESUMABLY	K. Hopelessness
___12. LUDICROUS	L. Looking pitiful, desperate or hopeless
___13. FUTILE	M. Inscription on a tombstone; summary of a deceased person's life
___14. DESPAIR	N. In a manner using statements or implications opposite to the underlying meaning
___15. PENETRATED	O. Religion of those who don't beleive in God and/or are uncivilized
___16. HAPHAZARDLY	P. Belief that minority cultures should dissolve into a dominant culture
___17. VENGEANCE	Q. In a manner befitting a woman who flirts with men
___18. REBUFFS	R. Overbearingly proud; haughty
___19. EPITAPH	S. Pierced; affected; diffused
___20. PLUNDER	T. Probably; reasonably supposed
___21. OMINOUS	U. Sorrowfully
___22. FORLORNLY	V. Menacing; threatening
___23. ASSIMILATIONISM	W. Without care; characterized by chance
___24. TYRANT	X. Ruler who exercises power in a harsh, cruel manner
___25. DESPERATION	Y. With violence or fury

A Raisin in the Sun Vocabulary Matching 1 Answer Key

N - 1. SARCASTICALLY	A. Violently; maliciously
E - 2. AMID	B. Irritated; provoked; irked
H - 3. INSINUATINGLY	C. To rob of goods by force; loot
U - 4. PLAINTIVELY	D. Laughably ridiculous
R - 5. ARROGANT	E. Among; in the midst of
O - 6. HEATHENISM	F. Condition of being driven to take almost any risk as a last resort
B - 7. EXASPERATED	G. Bluntly refuses
Q - 8. COQUETTISHLY	H. With more meaning than the spoken word; implying
J - 9. TENTATIVELY	I. Useless
A -10. VICIOUSLY	J. Uncertainly
T -11. PRESUMABLY	K. Hopelessness
D -12. LUDICROUS	L. Looking pitiful, desperate or hopeless
I - 13. FUTILE	M. Inscription on a tombstone; summary of a deceased person's life
K -14. DESPAIR	N. In a manner using statements or implications opposite to the underlying meaning
S -15. PENETRATED	O. Religion of those who don't beleive in God and/or are uncivilized
W -16. HAPHAZARDLY	P. Belief that minority cultures should dissolve into a dominant culture
Y -17. VENGEANCE	Q. In a manner befitting a woman who flirts with men
G -18. REBUFFS	R. Overbearingly proud; haughty
M -19. EPITAPH	S. Pierced; affected; diffused
C -20. PLUNDER	T. Probably; reasonably supposed
V -21. OMINOUS	U. Sorrowfully
L - 22. FORLORNLY	V. Menacing; threatening
P -23. ASSIMILATIONISM	W. Without care; characterized by chance
X -24. TYRANT	X. Ruler who exercises power in a harsh, cruel manner
F -25. DESPERATION	Y. With violence or fury

A Raisin in the Sun Vocabulary Matching 2

___ 1. CLICHE	A. Having unrestrained high spirtis; being overjoyed
___ 2. VICIOUSLY	B. Overbearingly proud; haughty
___ 3. HAPHAZARDLY	C. Stealthily; expressive of hidden motives
___ 4. FURTIVELY	D. Threateningly
___ 5. ARROGANT	E. Without care; characterized by chance
___ 6. PENETRATED	F. Shaped; made
___ 7. EXASPERATED	G. Trite or overused expression or idea
___ 8. SARCASTICALLY	H. In a manner using statements or implications opposite to the underlying meaning
___ 9. MUTILATED	I. In a manner befitting a woman who flirts with men
___10. DESPERATION	J. Laughably ridiculous
___11. EXUBERANCE	K. Tyrannical
___12. COQUETTISHLY	L. Religion of those who don't beleive in God and/or are uncivilized
___13. EPITAPH	M. Useless
___14. AMIABLY	N. Cleared of accusations, blame or suspicion
___15. UNDISTINGUISHED	O. Common; nothing special
___16. MENACINGLY	P. With violence or fury
___17. WROUGHT	Q. Maimed; damaged
___18. VINDICATED	R. Good naturedly
___19. LUDICROUS	S. Violently; maliciously
___20. FUTILE	T. Pierced; affected; diffused
___21. VENGEANCE	U. Condition of being driven to take almost any risk as a last resort
___22. OPPRESSIVE	V. Menacing; threatening
___23. OMINOUS	W. Irritated; provoked; irked
___24. HEATHENISM	X. Inscription on a tombstone; summary of a deceased person's life
___25. PLAINTIVELY	Y. Sorrowfully

A Raisin in the Sun Vocabulary Matching 2 Answer Key

G - 1. CLICHE	A. Having unrestrained high spirtis; being overjoyed
S - 2. VICIOUSLY	B. Overbearingly proud; haughty
E - 3. HAPHAZARDLY	C. Stealthily; expressive of hidden motives
C - 4. FURTIVELY	D. Threateningly
B - 5. ARROGANT	E. Without care; characterized by chance
T - 6. PENETRATED	F. Shaped; made
W - 7. EXASPERATED	G. Trite or overused expression or idea
H - 8. SARCASTICALLY	H. In a manner using statements or implications opposite to the underlying meaning
Q - 9. MUTILATED	I. In a manner befitting a woman who flirts with men
U -10. DESPERATION	J. Laughably ridiculous
A -11. EXUBERANCE	K. Tyrannical
I - 12. COQUETTISHLY	L. Religion of those who don't beleive in God and/or are uncivilized
X -13. EPITAPH	M. Useless
R -14. AMIABLY	N. Cleared of accusations, blame or suspicion
O -15. UNDISTINGUISHED	O. Common; nothing special
D -16. MENACINGLY	P. With violence or fury
F -17. WROUGHT	Q. Maimed; damaged
N -18. VINDICATED	R. Good naturedly
J - 19. LUDICROUS	S. Violently; maliciously
M -20. FUTILE	T. Pierced; affected; diffused
P -21. VENGEANCE	U. Condition of being driven to take almost any risk as a last resort
K -22. OPPRESSIVE	V. Menacing; threatening
V -23. OMINOUS	W. Irritated; provoked; irked
L - 24. HEATHENISM	X. Inscription on a tombstone; summary of a deceased person's life
Y -25. PLAINTIVELY	Y. Sorrowfully

A Raisin in the Sun Vocabulary Matching 3

___ 1. FURTIVELY	A. With more meaning than the spoken word; implying
___ 2. FORLORNLY	B. Suggested plan
___ 3. DESPERATION	C. Maimed; damaged
___ 4. INAPPROPRIATELY	D. Bluntly refuses
___ 5. HEATHENISM	E. Shaped; made
___ 6. SARCASTICALLY	F. Having unrestrained high spirtis; being overjoyed
___ 7. MONOLOGUE	G. Irritated; provoked; irked
___ 8. HAPHAZARDLY	H. Pierced; affected; diffused
___ 9. REBUFFS	I. Probably; reasonably supposed
___10. INSINUATINGLY	J. Without care; characterized by chance
___11. PLAINTIVELY	K. Condition of being driven to take almost any risk as a last resort
___12. MENACINGLY	L. In a manner using statements or implications opposite to the underlying meaning
___13. REVELATION	M. With violence or fury
___14. VENGEANCE	N. Common; nothing special
___15. OMINOUS	O. Sorrowfully
___16. MUTILATED	P. Menacing; threatening
___17. AMID	Q. Laughably ridiculous
___18. EXUBERANCE	R. Stealthily; expressive of hidden motives
___19. WROUGHT	S. Among; in the midst of
___20. PRESUMABLY	T. Looking pitiful, desperate or hopeless
___21. PENETRATED	U. Unsuitably; improperly
___22. PROPOSITION	V. Threateningly
___23. EXASPERATED	W. Long speech or talk made by one person
___24. UNDISTINGUISHED	X. Some new information; news
___25. LUDICROUS	Y. Religion of those who don't beleive in God and/or are uncivilized

A Raisin in the Sun Vocabulary Matching 3 Answer Key

R - 1. FURTIVELY	A. With more meaning than the spoken word; implying
T - 2. FORLORNLY	B. Suggested plan
K - 3. DESPERATION	C. Maimed; damaged
U - 4. INAPPROPRIATELY	D. Bluntly refuses
Y - 5. HEATHENISM	E. Shaped; made
L - 6. SARCASTICALLY	F. Having unrestrained high spirtis; being overjoyed
W - 7. MONOLOGUE	G. Irritated; provoked; irked
J - 8. HAPHAZARDLY	H. Pierced; affected; diffused
D - 9. REBUFFS	I. Probably; reasonably supposed
A -10. INSINUATINGLY	J. Without care; characterized by chance
O -11. PLAINTIVELY	K. Condition of being driven to take almost any risk as a last resort
V -12. MENACINGLY	L. In a manner using statements or implications opposite to the underlying meaning
X -13. REVELATION	M. With violence or fury
M -14. VENGEANCE	N. Common; nothing special
P -15. OMINOUS	O. Sorrowfully
C -16. MUTILATED	P. Menacing; threatening
S -17. AMID	Q. Laughably ridiculous
F -18. EXUBERANCE	R. Stealthily; expressive of hidden motives
E -19. WROUGHT	S. Among; in the midst of
I - 20. PRESUMABLY	T. Looking pitiful, desperate or hopeless
H -21. PENETRATED	U. Unsuitably; improperly
B -22. PROPOSITION	V. Threateningly
G -23. EXASPERATED	W. Long speech or talk made by one person
N -24. UNDISTINGUISHED	X. Some new information; news
Q -25. LUDICROUS	Y. Religion of those who don't beleive in God and/or are uncivilized

A Raisin in the Sun Vocabulary Matching 4

___ 1. MONOLOGUE	A. In a manner using statements or implications opposite to the underlying meaning
___ 2. TYRANT	B. Inscription on a tombstone; summary of a deceased person's life
___ 3. PROPOSITION	C. Some new information; news
___ 4. REVELATION	D. Hopelessness
___ 5. DESPAIR	E. Laughably ridiculous
___ 6. VENGEANCE	F. Common; nothing special
___ 7. COQUETTISHLY	G. In a manner befitting a woman who flirts with men
___ 8. EPITAPH	H. Pierced; affected; diffused
___ 9. PLUNDER	I. To rob of goods by force; loot
___10. LUDICROUS	J. Ruler who exercises power in a harsh, cruel manner
___11. ECCENTRIC	K. Cleared of accusations, blame or suspicion
___12. EXUBERANCE	L. Stealthily; expressive of hidden motives
___13. UNDISTINGUISHED	M. Shaped; made
___14. SARCASTICALLY	N. Bluntly refuses
___15. VICIOUSLY	O. Suggested plan
___16. WROUGHT	P. Deviating from the established norm, model or rule
___17. FURTIVELY	Q. Having unrestrained high spirtis; being overjoyed
___18. HEATHENISM	R. Religion of those who don't beleive in God and/or are uncivilized
___19. REBUFFS	S. Long speech or talk made by one person
___20. VINDICATED	T. Condition of being driven to take almost any risk as a last resort
___21. DESPERATION	U. Trite or overused expression or idea
___22. INSINUATINGLY	V. Violently; maliciously
___23. CLICHE	W. With more meaning than the spoken word; implying
___24. PENETRATED	X. With violence or fury
___25. PLAINTIVELY	Y. Sorrowfully

A Raisin in the Sun Vocabulary Matching 4 Answer Key

S - 1. MONOLOGUE	A. In a manner using statements or implications opposite to the underlying meaning
J - 2. TYRANT	B. Inscription on a tombstone; summary of a deceased person's life
O - 3. PROPOSITION	C. Some new information; news
C - 4. REVELATION	D. Hopelessness
D - 5. DESPAIR	E. Laughably ridiculous
X - 6. VENGEANCE	F. Common; nothing special
G - 7. COQUETTISHLY	G. In a manner befitting a woman who flirts with men
B - 8. EPITAPH	H. Pierced; affected; diffused
I - 9. PLUNDER	I. To rob of goods by force; loot
E -10. LUDICROUS	J. Ruler who exercises power in a harsh, cruel manner
P -11. ECCENTRIC	K. Cleared of accusations, blame or suspicion
Q -12. EXUBERANCE	L. Stealthily; expressive of hidden motives
F -13. UNDISTINGUISHED	M. Shaped; made
A -14. SARCASTICALLY	N. Bluntly refuses
V -15. VICIOUSLY	O. Suggested plan
M -16. WROUGHT	P. Deviating from the established norm, model or rule
L -17. FURTIVELY	Q. Having unrestrained high spirtis; being overjoyed
R -18. HEATHENISM	R. Religion of those who don't beleive in God and/or are uncivilized
N -19. REBUFFS	S. Long speech or talk made by one person
K -20. VINDICATED	T. Condition of being driven to take almost any risk as a last resort
T -21. DESPERATION	U. Trite or overused expression or idea
W -22. INSINUATINGLY	V. Violently; maliciously
U -23. CLICHE	W. With more meaning than the spoken word; implying
H -24. PENETRATED	X. With violence or fury
Y -25. PLAINTIVELY	Y. Sorrowfully

A Raisin in the Sun Vocabulary Magic Squares 1

Match the definition with the vocabulary word. Put your answers in the magic squares below. When your answers are correct, all columns and rows will add to the same number.

A. VINDICATED
B. TYRANT
C. REBUFFS
D. ASSIMILATIONISM
E. OPPRESSIVE
F. EXASPERATED
G. VENGEANCE
H. PLUNDER
I. INAPPROPRIATELY
J. REVELATION
K. AMIABLY
L. FURTIVELY
M. EXUBERANCE
N. TENTATIVELY
O. AMID
P. CLICHE

1. Having unrestrained high spirtis; being overjoyed
2. Irritated; provoked; irked
3. To rob of goods by force; loot
4. Among; in the midst of
5. Stealthily; expressive of hidden motives
6. Bluntly refuses
7. Cleared of accusations, blame or suspicion
8. Some new information; news
9. Good naturedly
10. Belief that minority cultures should dissolve into a dominant culture
11. Ruler who exercises power in a harsh, cruel manner
12. Unsuitably; improperly
13. Uncertainly
14. Tyrannical
15. With violence or fury
16. Trite or overused expression or idea

A=	B=	C=	D=
E=	F=	G=	H=
I=	J=	K=	L=
M=	N=	O=	P=

A Raisin in the Sun Vocabulary Magic Squares 1 Answer Key

Match the definition with the vocabulary word. Put your answers in the magic squares below. When your answers are correct, all columns and rows will add to the same number.

A. VINDICATED
B. TYRANT
C. REBUFFS
D. ASSIMILATIONISM
E. OPPRESSIVE
F. EXASPERATED
G. VENGEANCE
H. PLUNDER
I. INAPPROPRIATELY
J. REVELATION
K. AMIABLY
L. FURTIVELY
M. EXUBERANCE
N. TENTATIVELY
O. AMID
P. CLICHE

1. Having unrestrained high spirtis; being overjoyed
2. Irritated; provoked; irked
3. To rob of goods by force; loot
4. Among; in the midst of
5. Stealthily; expressive of hidden motives
6. Bluntly refuses
7. Cleared of accusations, blame or suspicion
8. Some new information; news
9. Good naturedly
10. Belief that minority cultures should dissolve into a dominant culture
11. Ruler who exercises power in a harsh, cruel manner
12. Unsuitably; improperly
13. Uncertainly
14. Tyrannical
15. With violence or fury
16. Trite or overused expression or idea

A=7	B=11	C=6	D=10
E=14	F=2	G=15	H=3
I=12	J=8	K=9	L=5
M=1	N=13	O=4	P=16

A Raisin in the Sun Vocabulary Magic Squares 2

Match the definition with the vocabulary word. Put your answers in the magic squares below. When your answers are correct, all columns and rows will add to the same number.

A. TYRANT
B. DESPAIR
C. EXASPERATED
D. COQUETTISHLY
E. AMID
F. VINDICATED
G. MUTILATED
H. OPPRESSIVE
I. CLICHE
J. ASSIMILATIONISM
K. OMINOUS
L. PROPOSITION
M. EPITAPH
N. PRESUMABLY
O. PENETRATED
P. HAPHAZARDLY

1. Tyrannical
2. Inscription on a tombstone; summary of a deceased person's life
3. Hopelessness
4. Menacing; threatening
5. Belief that minority cultures should dissolve into a dominant culture
6. Irritated; provoked; irked
7. Without care; characterized by chance
8. Among; in the midst of
9. Pierced; affected; diffused
10. Cleared of accusations, blame or suspicion
11. Trite or overused expression or idea
12. In a manner befitting a woman who flirts with men
13. Ruler who exercises power in a harsh, cruel manner
14. Suggested plan
15. Maimed; damaged
16. Probably; reasonably supposed

A=	B=	C=	D=
E=	F=	G=	H=
I=	J=	K=	L=
M=	N=	O=	P=

A Raisin in the Sun Vocabulary Magic Squares 2 Answer Key

Match the definition with the vocabulary word. Put your answers in the magic squares below. When your answers are correct, all columns and rows will add to the same number.

A. TYRANT
B. DESPAIR
C. EXASPERATED
D. COQUETTISHLY
E. AMID
F. VINDICATED
G. MUTILATED
H. OPPRESSIVE
I. CLICHE
J. ASSIMILATIONISM
K. OMINOUS
L. PROPOSITION
M. EPITAPH
N. PRESUMABLY
O. PENETRATED
P. HAPHAZARDLY

1. Tyrannical
2. Inscription on a tombstone; summary of a deceased person's life
3. Hopelessness
4. Menacing; threatening
5. Belief that minority cultures should dissolve into a dominant culture
6. Irritated; provoked; irked
7. Without care; characterized by chance
8. Among; in the midst of
9. Pierced; affected; diffused
10. Cleared of accusations, blame or suspicion
11. Trite or overused expression or idea
12. In a manner befitting a woman who flirts with men
13. Ruler who exercises power in a harsh, cruel manner
14. Suggested plan
15. Maimed; damaged
16. Probably; reasonably supposed

A=13	B=3	C=6	D=12
E=8	F=10	G=15	H=1
I=11	J=5	K=4	L=14
M=2	N=16	O=9	P=7

A Raisin in the Sun Vocabulary Magic Squares 3

Match the definition with the vocabulary word. Put your answers in the magic squares below. When your answers are correct, all columns and rows will add to the same number.

A. PLUNDER
B. OMINOUS
C. UNDISTINGUISHED
D. DESPAIR
E. VINDICATED
F. EXASPERATED
G. SARCASTICALLY
H. LUDICROUS
I. MONOLOGUE
J. PENETRATED
K. REVELATION
L. AMID
M. REBUFFS
N. AMIABLY
O. HAPHAZARDLY
P. OPPRESSIVE

1. Without care; characterized by chance
2. Pierced; affected; diffused
3. Laughably ridiculous
4. To rob of goods by force; loot
5. Hopelessness
6. Cleared of accusations, blame or suspicion
7. Some new information; news
8. Good naturedly
9. Irritated; provoked; irked
10. Common; nothing special
11. Bluntly refuses
12. Among; in the midst of
13. Long speech or talk made by one person
14. Tyrannical
15. Menacing; threatening
16. In a manner using statements or implications opposite to the underlying meaning

A=	B=	C=	D=
E=	F=	G=	H=
I=	J=	K=	L=
M=	N=	O=	P=

A Raisin in the Sun Vocabulary Magic Squares 3 Answer Key

Match the definition with the vocabulary word. Put your answers in the magic squares below. When your answers are correct, all columns and rows will add to the same number.

A. PLUNDER
B. OMINOUS
C. UNDISTINGUISHED
D. DESPAIR
E. VINDICATED
F. EXASPERATED
G. SARCASTICALLY
H. LUDICROUS
I. MONOLOGUE
J. PENETRATED
K. REVELATION
L. AMID
M. REBUFFS
N. AMIABLY
O. HAPHAZARDLY
P. OPPRESSIVE

1. Without care; characterized by chance
2. Pierced; affected; diffused
3. Laughably ridiculous
4. To rob of goods by force; loot
5. Hopelessness
6. Cleared of accusations, blame or suspicion
7. Some new information; news
8. Good naturedly
9. Irritated; provoked; irked
10. Common; nothing special
11. Bluntly refuses
12. Among; in the midst of
13. Long speech or talk made by one person
14. Tyrannical
15. Menacing; threatening
16. In a manner using statements or implications opposite to the underlying meaning

A=4	B=15	C=10	D=5
E=6	F=9	G=16	H=3
I=13	J=2	K=7	L=12
M=11	N=8	O=1	P=14

A Raisin in the Sun Vocabulary Magic Squares 4

Match the definition with the vocabulary word. Put your answers in the magic squares below. When your answers are correct, all columns and rows will add to the same number.

A. FORLORNLY
B. ARROGANT
C. INSINUATINGLY
D. CLICHE
E. FURTIVELY
F. PRESUMABLY
G. EXASPERATED
H. TYRANT
I. HEATHENISM
J. VENGEANCE
K. DESPERATION
L. AMIABLY
M. OPPRESSIVE
N. LUDICROUS
O. PROPOSITION
P. PENETRATED

1. Looking pitiful, desperate or hopeless
2. Laughably ridiculous
3. With violence or fury
4. Stealthily; expressive of hidden motives
5. Irritated; provoked; irked
6. Good naturedly
7. Pierced; affected; diffused
8. With more meaning than the spoken word; implying
9. Suggested plan
10. Trite or overused expression or idea
11. Ruler who exercises power in a harsh, cruel manner
12. Condition of being driven to take almost any risk as a last resort
13. Religion of those who don't beleive in God and/or are uncivilized
14. Probably; reasonably supposed
15. Overbearingly proud; haughty
16. Tyrannical

A=	B=	C=	D=
E=	F=	G=	H=
I=	J=	K=	L=
M=	N=	O=	P=

A Raisin in the Sun Vocabulary Magic Squares 4 Answer Key

Match the definition with the vocabulary word. Put your answers in the magic squares below. When your answers are correct, all columns and rows will add to the same number.

A. FORLORNLY
B. ARROGANT
C. INSINUATINGLY
D. CLICHE
E. FURTIVELY
F. PRESUMABLY
G. EXASPERATED
H. TYRANT
I. HEATHENISM
J. VENGEANCE
K. DESPERATION
L. AMIABLY
M. OPPRESSIVE
N. LUDICROUS
O. PROPOSITION
P. PENETRATED

1. Looking pitiful, desperate or hopeless
2. Laughably ridiculous
3. With violence or fury
4. Stealthily; expressive of hidden motives
5. Irritated; provoked; irked
6. Good naturedly
7. Pierced; affected; diffused
8. With more meaning than the spoken word; implying
9. Suggested plan
10. Trite or overused expression or idea
11. Ruler who exercises power in a harsh, cruel manner
12. Condition of being driven to take almost any risk as a last resort
13. Religion of those who don't beleive in God and/or are uncivilized
14. Probably; reasonably supposed
15. Overbearingly proud; haughty
16. Tyrannical

A=1	B=15	C=8	D=10
E=4	F=14	G=5	H=11
I=13	J=3	K=12	L=6
M=16	N=2	O=9	P=7

A Raisin in the Sun Vocabulary Word Search 1

Words are placed backwards, forward, diagonally, up and down. Clues listed below can help you find the words. Circle the hidden vocabulary words in the maze.

L	S	A	R	C	A	S	T	I	C	A	L	L	Y	Y	Z	E	L	M	P
U	Y	L	E	V	I	T	A	T	N	E	T	L	L	K	C	T	T	O	N
D	B	Q	V	I	F	F	P	F	Z	C	S	E	B	N	R	V	Y	N	T
I	P	Y	E	N	L	U	P	P	V	U	V	W	A	Z	C	S	E	O	F
C	S	R	L	D	N	G	T	F	O	I	F	R	M	M	K	C	Z	L	W
R	W	V	A	I	Y	R	R	I	T	K	E	C	U	H	N	P	P	O	V
O	F	T	T	C	H	D	C	R	L	B	L	T	S	A	T	L	M	G	H
U	H	F	I	A	V	I	U	X	U	E	I	Z	E	H	Y	A	S	U	P
S	Z	E	O	T	V	F	Q	X	V	L	W	G	R	J	R	I	I	E	N
R	C	X	N	E	G	X	E	X	A	D	N	S	P	O	A	N	N	W	Q
J	C	A	T	D	T	J	W	T	Z	E	D	S	H	M	N	T	E	R	R
P	E	S	F	F	U	B	E	R	V	S	S	Z	J	I	T	I	H	O	X
R	C	P	K	T	B	D	Y	S	W	P	P	B	O	N	F	V	T	U	S
O	C	E	L	T	T	Y	V	W	D	A	W	P	K	O	V	E	A	G	H
P	E	R	V	N	D	K	B	W	D	I	P	G	R	U	C	L	E	H	B
O	N	A	H	A	P	H	A	Z	A	R	D	L	Y	S	Y	Y	H	T	R
S	T	T	N	G	D	T	Z	W	E	T	O	X	C	L	X	P	V	E	D
I	R	E	Y	O	H	H	C	S	C	R	A	K	B	D	A	G	D	T	X
T	I	D	F	R	G	Q	S	J	N	V	M	A	P	T	G	N	B	Q	G
I	C	J	F	R	L	I	R	L	N	G	I	H	I	C	U	D	X	Q	D
O	X	G	T	A	V	B	Y	Y	Q	M	D	P	F	L	L	L	S	L	V
N	P	R	P	E	N	E	T	R	A	T	E	D	P	C	L	I	C	H	E

Among; in the midst of (4)
Bluntly refuses (7)
Cleared of accusations, blame or suspicion (10)
Deviating from the established norm, model or rule (9)
Good naturedly (7)
Having unrestrained high spirtis; being overjoyed (10)
Hopelessness (7)
In a manner using statements or implications opposite to the underlying meaning (13)
Inscription on a tombstone; summary of a deceased person's life (7)
Irritated; provoked; irked (11)
Laughably ridiculous (9)
Long speech or talk made by one person (9)
Looking pitiful, desperate or hopeless (9)
Maimed; damaged (9)
Menacing; threatening (7)
Overbearingly proud; haughty (8)
Pierced; affected; diffused (10)
Probably; reasonably supposed (10)
Religion of those who don't beleive in God and/or are uncivilized (10)
Ruler who exercises power in a harsh, cruel manner (6)
Shaped; made (7)
Some new information; news (10)
Sorrowfully (11)
Stealthily; expressive of hidden motives (9)
Suggested plan (11)
To rob of goods by force; loot (7)
Trite or overused expression or idea (6)
Tyrannical (10)
Uncertainly (11)
Useless (6)
Violently; maliciously (9)
With violence or fury (9)
Without care; characterized by chance (11)

A Raisin in the Sun Vocabulary Word Search 1 Answer Key

Words are placed backwards, forward, diagonally, up and down. Clues listed below can help you find the words. Circle the hidden vocabulary words in the maze.

L	S	A	R	C	A	S	T	I	C	A	L	L	Y	Y		E		M	
U	Y	L	E	V	I	T	A	T	N	E	T	L	L		C			O	
D			V	I	F						S	E	B	N				N	
I			E	N		U				U	V		A				E	O	
C			L	D			T		O	I		R	M	M		C		L	
R			A	I				I	T		E		U		N	P		O	
O			T	C			C	R	L	B		T	S	A	T	L	M	G	
U			I	A		I	U		U	E	I		E		Y	A	S	U	
S		E	O	T	V	F		X		L		G	R		R	I	I	E	
		X	N	E			E		A	D	N		P	O	A	N	N	W	
		A		D				T		E				M	N	T	E	R	
P	E	S	F	F	U	B	E	R	V	S				I	T	I	H	O	
R	C	P				D				P			O	N	F	V	T	U	
O	C	E		T						A		P		O		E	A	G	
P	E	R		N						I	P		R	U		L	E	H	
O	N	A	H	A	P	H	A	Z	A	R	D	L	Y	S	Y	Y	H	T	R
S	T	T		G					E		O			L		P		E	
I	R	E		O				S		R	A		B		A		D		
T	I	D		R			S		N		M	A		T		N			
I	C			R		I		L			I		I		U				
O				A	V		Y			M	D	P		L					
N			P	E	N	E	T	R	A	T	E	D	P	C	L	I	C	H	E

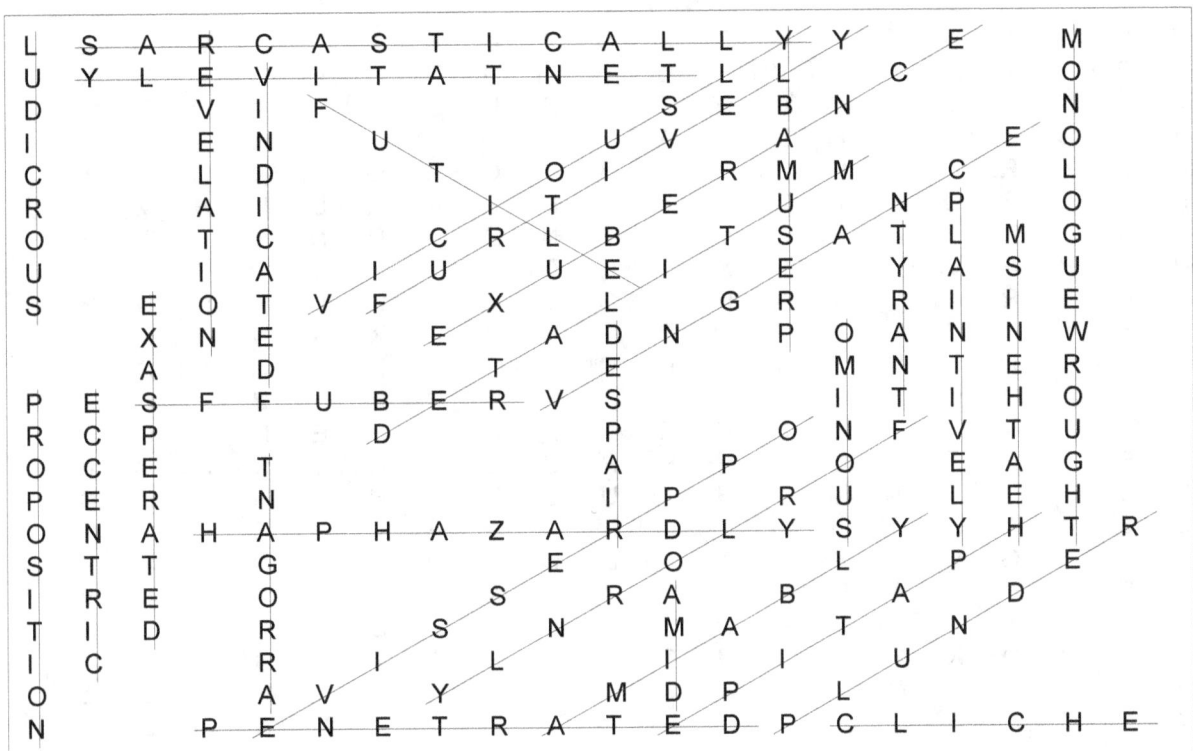

Among; in the midst of (4)
Bluntly refuses (7)
Cleared of accusations, blame or suspicion (10)
Deviating from the established norm, model or rule (9)
Good naturedly (7)
Having unrestrained high spirtis; being overjoyed (10)
Hopelessness (7)
In a manner using statements or implications opposite to the underlying meaning (13)
Inscription on a tombstone; summary of a deceased person's life (7)
Irritated; provoked; irked (11)
Laughably ridiculous (9)
Long speech or talk made by one person (9)
Looking pitiful, desperate or hopeless (9)
Maimed; damaged (9)
Menacing; threatening (7)
Overbearingly proud; haughty (8)
Pierced; affected; diffused (10)
Probably; reasonably supposed (10)
Religion of those who don't beleive in God and/or are uncivilized (10)
Ruler who exercises power in a harsh, cruel manner (6)
Shaped; made (7)
Some new information; news (10)
Sorrowfully (11)
Stealthily; expressive of hidden motives (9)
Suggested plan (11)
To rob of goods by force; loot (7)
Trite or overused expression or idea (6)
Tyrannical (10)
Uncertainly (11)
Useless (6)
Violently; maliciously (9)
With violence or fury (9)
Without care; characterized by chance (11)

A Raisin in the Sun Vocabulary Word Search 2

Words are placed backwards, forward, diagonally, up and down. Clues listed below can help you find the words. Circle the hidden vocabulary words in the maze.

H	E	A	T	H	E	N	I	S	M	O	Z	B	F	T	R	J	W	M	L
T	E	N	T	A	T	I	V	E	L	Y	M	U	X	N	W	Q	R	U	X
V	E	N	G	E	A	N	C	E	T	L	R	I	T	A	W	U	O	T	J
M	N	C	D	E	S	P	E	R	A	T	I	O	N	G	L	N	U	I	V
S	R	Z	R	F	L	P	P	Y	I	B	K	O	A	O	D	D	G	L	J
B	Z	Q	F	D	I	V	L	V	Z	V	I	S	R	R	U	I	H	A	Z
A	M	I	D	T	B	S	E	V	W	T	N	Z	Y	R	N	S	T	T	B
M	K	P	A	W	U	L	C	X	A	F	D	B	T	A	C	T	F	E	R
F	O	P	R	O	Y	M	A	L	U	Q	B	Z	J	K	I	I	U	D	B
Y	H	N	I	O	S	B	E	M	P	B	H	P	N	X	R	N	T	J	H
B	T	C	O	R	P	V	X	E	I	Q	E	C	C	P	T	G	I	C	Q
T	I	O	W	L	E	O	N	K	X	A	H	R	R	R	N	U	L	F	Z
V	L	Q	V	R	O	E	S	V	G	A	B	E	A	F	E	I	E	O	C
D	P	U	G	F	T	G	G	I	P	P	S	L	N	N	C	S	P	R	V
P	L	E	D	R	M	M	U	H	T	U	L	P	Y	H	C	H	R	L	C
L	B	T	A	I	W	H	A	E	M	I	Q	V	E	J	E	E	I	O	M
U	P	T	G	V	C	Z	V	A	H	L	O	N	D	R	B	D	A	R	Y
N	E	I	C	B	A	R	B	L	B	K	L	N	M	U	A	W	P	N	R
D	S	S	T	R	D	L	O	Q	X	S	P	Y	F	Z	N	T	S	L	K
E	D	H	D	X	Y	T	V	U	D	K	K	F	J	T	K	S	E	Y	P
R	Z	L	Y	L	M	Y	F	X	S	D	S	X	R	S	M	F	D	D	Z
Y	Y	Y	A	S	S	I	M	I	L	A	T	I	O	N	I	S	M	D	Y

Among; in the midst of (4)
Belief that minority cultures should dissolve into a dominant culture (15)
Bluntly refuses (7)
Common; nothing special (15)
Condition of being driven to take almost any risk as a last resort (11)
Deviating from the established norm, model or rule (9)
Good naturedly (7)
Having unrestrained high spirtis; being overjoyed (10)
Hopelessness (7)
In a manner befitting a woman who flirts with men (12)
Inscription on a tombstone; summary of a deceased person's life (7)
Irritated; provoked; irked (11)
Laughably ridiculous (9)
Long speech or talk made by one person (9)
Looking pitiful, desperate or hopeless (9)
Maimed; damaged (9)
Menacing; threatening (7)
Overbearingly proud; haughty (8)
Pierced; affected; diffused (10)
Probably; reasonably supposed (10)
Religion of those who don't beleive in God and/or are uncivilized (10)
Ruler who exercises power in a harsh, cruel manner (6)
Shaped; made (7)
Some new information; news (10)
Stealthily; expressive of hidden motives (9)
Suggested plan (11)
To rob of goods by force; loot (7)
Trite or overused expression or idea (6)
Uncertainly (11)
Useless (6)
Violently; maliciously (9)
With violence or fury (9)
Without care; characterized by chance (11)

A Raisin in the Sun Vocabulary Word Search 2 Answer Key

Words are placed backwards, forward, diagonally, up and down. Clues listed below can help you find the words. Circle the hidden vocabulary words in the maze.

H	E	A	T	H	E	N	I	S	M	O			F	T			W	M
T	E	N	T	A	T	I	V	E	L	Y	M	U		N			R	U
V	E	N	G	E	A	N	C	E			R	I	T	A		U	O	T
			D	E	S	P	E	R	A	T	I	O	N	G		N	U	I
						P		Y	I			O	A	O		D	G	L
					I		L	V			I		R	R	U	I	H	A
A	M	I	D	T		S	E			T			Y	R		S	T	T
M		P	A		U	L		X	A				T	A	C	T	F	E
	O	P	R	O	Y		A	L	U						I	I	U	D
	H	N	I	O			E	M	P	B					R	N	T	
		C	O		P	V		E	I		E			P	T	G	I	C
	I	O		L	E	O	N		X	A	H	R	R		N	U	L	F
V	L	Q		R	O	E	S			A	B	E	A		E	I	E	O
		U			T	G		I	P		S	L		N	C	S		R
P		E	D	R			U	H	T	U		P	Y	H	C	H	R	L
L		T	A	I			A	E	M	I			E		E	E	I	O
U		T			C	Z		A			O			R	B	D	A	R
N	E	I			A	R	B					N		U	A		P	N
D		S		R		L	O						F			T	S	L
E		H	D		Y			U				F					E	Y
R		L							S		S						D	D
	Y	Y	A	S	S	I	M	I	L	A	T	I	O	N	I	S	M	

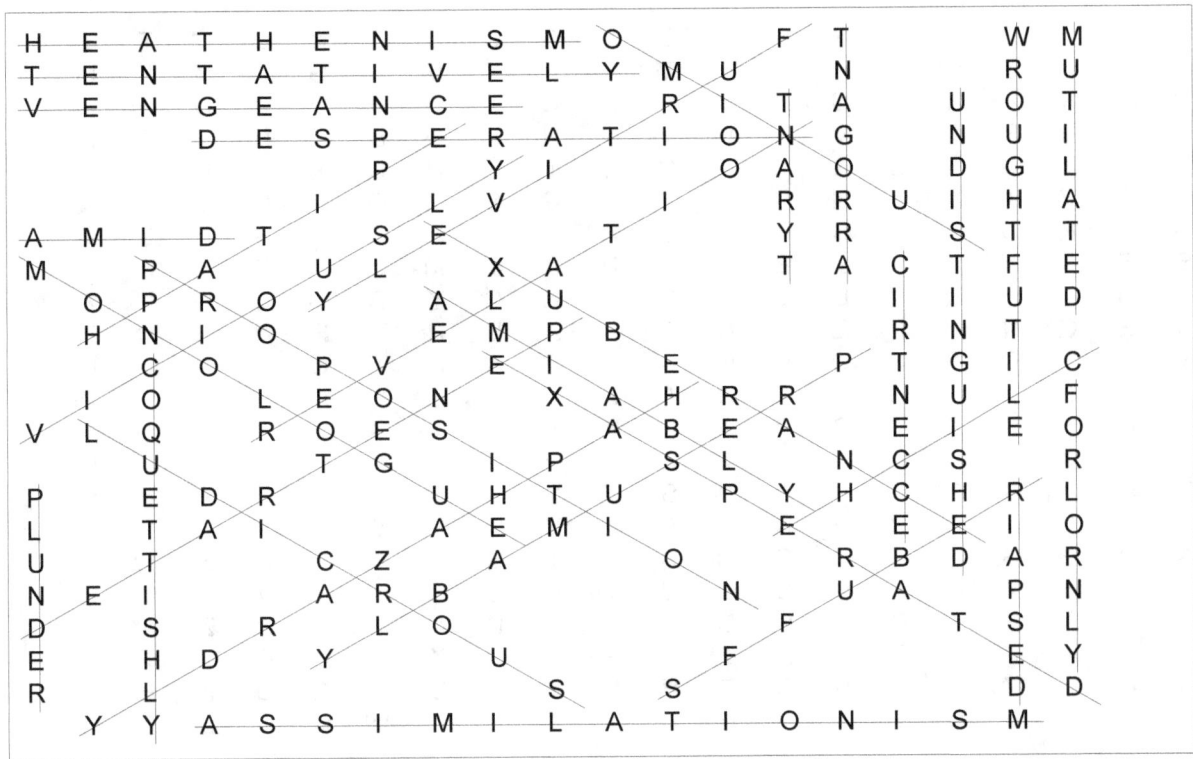

Among; in the midst of (4)
Belief that minority cultures should dissolve into a dominant culture (15)
Bluntly refuses (7)
Common; nothing special (15)
Condition of being driven to take almost any risk as a last resort (11)
Deviating from the established norm, model or rule (9)
Good naturedly (7)
Having unrestrained high spirtis; being overjoyed (10)
Hopelessness (7)
In a manner befitting a woman who flirts with men (12)
Inscription on a tombstone; summary of a deceased person's life (7)
Irritated; provoked; irked (11)
Laughably ridiculous (9)
Long speech or talk made by one person (9)
Looking pitiful, desperate or hopeless (9)
Maimed; damaged (9)
Menacing; threatening (7)
Overbearingly proud; haughty (8)
Pierced; affected; diffused (10)
Probably; reasonably supposed (10)
Religion of those who don't beleive in God and/or are uncivilized (10)
Ruler who exercises power in a harsh, cruel manner (6)
Shaped; made (7)
Some new information; news (10)
Stealthily; expressive of hidden motives (9)
Suggested plan (11)
To rob of goods by force; loot (7)
Trite or overused expression or idea (6)
Uncertainly (11)
Useless (6)
Violently; maliciously (9)
With violence or fury (9)
Without care; characterized by chance (11)

A Raisin in the Sun Vocabulary Word Search 3

Words are placed backwards, forward, diagonally, up and down. Words listed below are included in the maze. Circle the hidden vocabulary words in the maze.

O	P	P	R	E	S	S	I	V	E	U	G	O	L	O	N	O	M	T	T
Y	L	G	N	I	C	A	N	E	M	M	B	Y	V	N	G	W	Y	F	M
P	V	K	Z	L	K	C	K	V	L	J	Q	X	O	H	D	P	D	T	G
L	F	U	R	T	I	V	E	L	Y	J	N	I	Q	E	K	M	Y	B	R
U	E	X	U	B	E	R	A	N	C	E	T	K	H	C	X	V	L	D	N
N	T	V	J	X	H	H	B	F	T	A	G	S	Y	O	D	C	E	F	N
D	P	P	O	H	L	S	P	D	L	R	I	S	Z	Q	R	S	T	C	W
E	E	C	M	V	J	J	E	E	T	U	I	J	M	U	P	X	A	L	P
R	N	J	I	Q	V	L	V	J	G	V	K	C	Y	E	M	C	I	I	Z
K	E	Q	N	M	I	E	W	N	G	R	Z	L	R	T	F	N	R	C	Z
Y	T	L	O	T	R	Q	I	F	B	N	G	A	D	T	O	R	P	H	L
W	R	O	U	G	H	T	Y	R	A	N	T	T	E	I	R	E	O	E	W
K	A	F	S	D	S	B	R	J	I	I	Y	R	T	S	L	B	R	V	Y
A	T	V	G	I	I	Z	F	T	O	L	P	I	A	H	O	U	P	I	K
M	E	E	D	A	Z	C	A	N	S	K	S	A	R	L	R	F	P	N	S
I	D	N	J	P	R	U	R	U	A	O	Y	P	E	Y	N	F	A	D	L
A	U	G	G	Y	N	R	O	O	P	M	T	S	P	Z	L	S	N	I	F
B	Z	E	Y	I	F	I	O	O	U	W	I	E	S	P	Y	V	I	C	Q
L	N	A	S	K	C	Q	R	G	R	S	V	D	A	Y	H	R	Z	A	Z
Y	D	N	W	I	E	P	I	T	A	P	H	D	X	F	Z	C	Z	T	Q
X	I	C	V	G	L	H	C	P	H	N	Y	J	E	G	Q	D	K	E	C
Y	L	E	V	I	T	A	T	N	E	T	T	Z	C	W	C	C	L	D	Z

AMIABLY
AMID
ARROGANT
CLICHE
COQUETTISHLY
DESPAIR
DESPERATION
ECCENTRIC
EPITAPH
EXASPERATED
EXUBERANCE

FORLORNLY
FURTIVELY
FUTILE
INAPPROPRIATELY
INSINUATINGLY
LUDICROUS
MENACINGLY
MONOLOGUE
OMINOUS
OPPRESSIVE
PENETRATED

PLUNDER
PROPOSITION
REBUFFS
REVELATION
TENTATIVELY
TYRANT
UNDISTINGUISHED
VENGEANCE
VICIOUSLY
VINDICATED
WROUGHT

A Raisin in the Sun Vocabulary Word Search 3 Answer Key

Words are placed backwards, forward, diagonally, up and down. Words listed below are included in the maze. Circle the hidden vocabulary words in the maze.

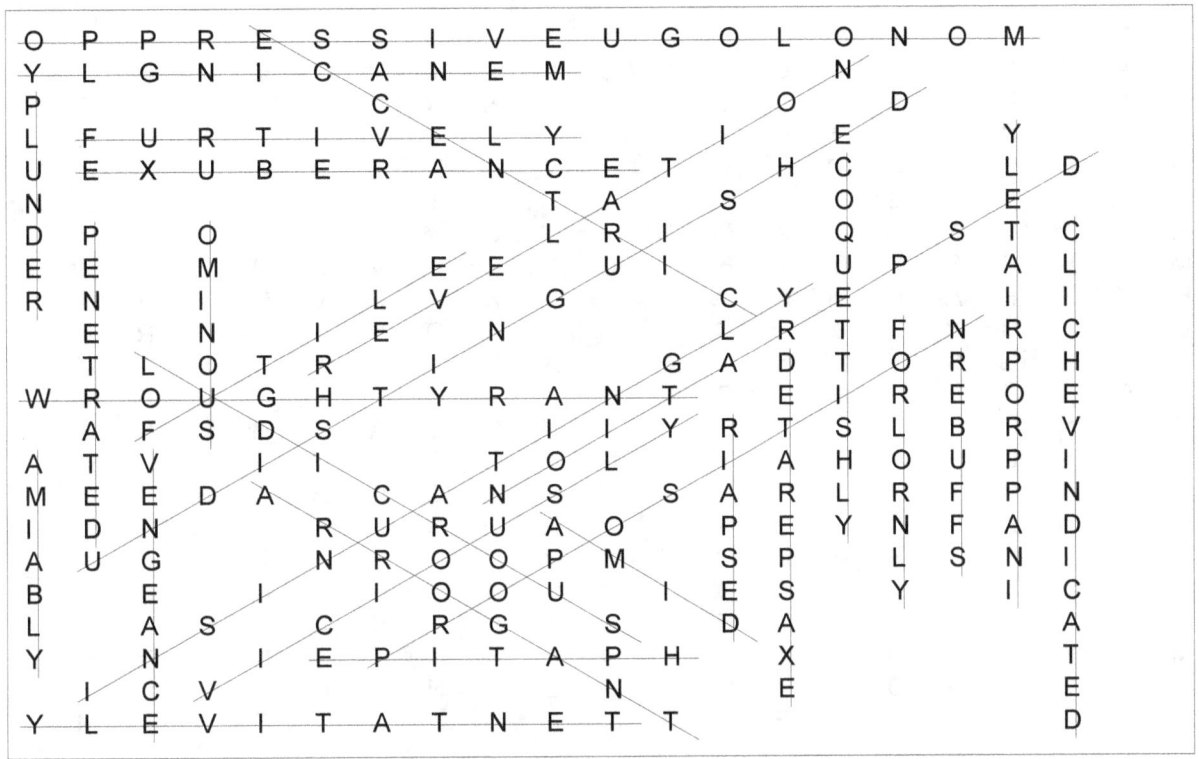

O	P	P	R	E	S	S	I	V	E	U	G	O	L	O	N	O	M	
Y	L	G	N	I	C	A	N	E	M					N				
P						C							O		D			
L	F	U	R	T	I	V	E	L	Y			I		E			Y	
U	E	X	U	B	E	R	A	N	C	E	T		H	C			L	D
N									T	A		S		O			E	
D	P		O						L	R	I			Q		S	T	C
E	E		M				E	E		U	I			U	P		A	L
R	N		I			L	V		G			C	Y	E			I	I
	E		N		I	E		N				L	R	T	F	N	R	C
	T	L	O	T	R		I				G	A	D	T	O	R	P	H
W	R	O	U	G	H	T	Y	R	A	N	T		E	I	R	E	O	E
	A	F	S	D	S				I	I	Y	R	T	S	L	B	R	V
A	T	V		I	I			T	O	L		I	A	H	O	U	P	I
M	E	E	D	A		C	A	N	S		S	A	R	L	R	F	P	N
I	D	N			R	U	R	U	A	O		P	E	Y	N	F	A	D
A	U	G			N	R	O	O	P	M		S	P		L	S	N	I
B		E		I		I	O	O	U		I	E	S		Y		I	C
L		A	S		C		R	G		S		D	A					A
Y		N		I	E	P	I	T	A	P	H		X					T
	I	C	V							N			E					E
Y	L	E	V	I	T	A	T	N	E	T	T							D

AMIABLY

AMID

ARROGANT

CLICHE

COQUETTISHLY

DESPAIR

DESPERATION

ECCENTRIC

EPITAPH

EXASPERATED

EXUBERANCE

FORLORNLY

FURTIVELY

FUTILE

INAPPROPRIATELY

INSINUATINGLY

LUDICROUS

MENACINGLY

MONOLOGUE

OMINOUS

OPPRESSIVE

PENETRATED

PLUNDER

PROPOSITION

REBUFFS

REVELATION

TENTATIVELY

TYRANT

UNDISTINGUISHED

VENGEANCE

VICIOUSLY

VINDICATED

WROUGHT

A Raisin in the Sun Vocabulary Word Search 4

Words are placed backwards, forward, diagonally, up and down. Words listed below are included in the maze. Circle the hidden vocabulary words in the maze.

P	O	P	P	R	E	S	S	I	V	E	T	F	U	T	I	L	E	C	B
L	X	R	F	O	R	L	O	R	N	L	Y	Y	Y	R	K	C	P	S	S
U	T	E	N	T	A	T	I	V	E	L	Y	H	R	V	N	P	U	D	S
N	K	S	S	N	Q	P	L	W	M	M	J	B	B	A	C	O	H	Z	R
D	W	U	F	U	R	T	I	V	E	L	Y	M	P	D	N	A	M	I	D
E	L	M	Y	N	G	P	G	N	P	L	L	Y	J	I	D	T	A	N	B
R	J	A	B	N	H	F	A	M	D	Y	G	S	M	T	J	P	H	A	R
M	R	B	B	G	P	C	Y	R	R	L	N	O	R	V	S	W	E	P	W
R	Y	L	B	A	I	M	A	W	E	S	I	Z	P	E	V	R	A	P	Y
E	E	Y	B	N	X	Z	Q	C	C	U	T	L	D	N	I	O	T	R	Y
P	C	V	G	S	A	F	N	Q	C	O	A	U	P	G	N	U	H	O	M
I	E	L	E	H	J	A	J	D	E	I	U	D	R	E	D	G	E	P	Y
T	Y	N	P	L	R	C	E	J	N	C	N	I	O	A	I	H	N	R	B
A	L	A	E	E	A	T	C	T	T	I	I	C	P	N	C	T	I	I	W
P	H	Y	B	T	A	T	I	P	R	V	S	R	O	C	A	S	S	A	R
H	Y	U	K	L	R	V	I	S	I	M	N	O	S	E	T	Q	M	T	G
X	X	C	I	K	E	A	F	O	C	Y	I	U	I	P	E	Z	W	E	B
E	H	T	L	L	K	F	T	D	N	S	N	S	T	C	D	G	L	L	X
T	U	X	Y	I	U	K	T	E	V	Q	Y	V	I	K	D	B	F	Y	F
M	G	H	T	B	C	F	R	K	D	A	R	R	O	G	A	N	T	R	K
S	R	G	E	B	D	H	E	U	G	O	L	O	N	O	M	W	G	S	F
V	G	R	D	E	S	P	E	R	A	T	I	O	N	D	G	G	S	L	M

AMIABLY

AMID

ARROGANT

CLICHE

DESPAIR

DESPERATION

ECCENTRIC

EPITAPH

EXUBERANCE

FORLORNLY

FURTIVELY

FUTILE

HAPHAZARDLY

HEATHENISM

INAPPROPRIATELY

INSINUATINGLY

LUDICROUS

MENACINGLY

MONOLOGUE

MUTILATED

OMINOUS

OPPRESSIVE

PENETRATED

PLAINTIVELY

PLUNDER

PRESUMABLY

PROPOSITION

REBUFFS

REVELATION

TENTATIVELY

TYRANT

VENGEANCE

VICIOUSLY

VINDICATED

WROUGHT

A Raisin in the Sun Vocabulary Word Search 4 Answer Key

Words are placed backwards, forward, diagonally, up and down. Words listed below are included in the maze. Circle the hidden vocabulary words in the maze.

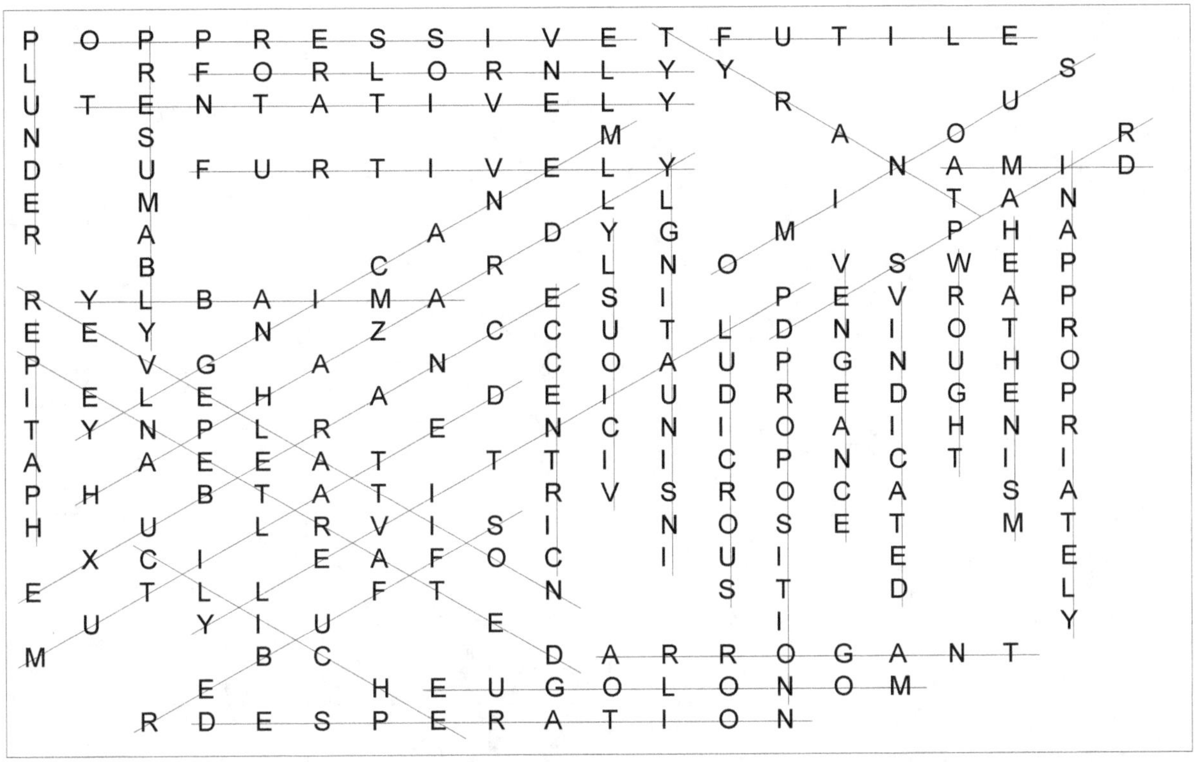

AMIABLY

AMID

ARROGANT

CLICHE

DESPAIR

DESPERATION

ECCENTRIC

EPITAPH

EXUBERANCE

FORLORNLY

FURTIVELY

FUTILE

HAPHAZARDLY

HEATHENISM

INAPPROPRIATELY

INSINUATINGLY

LUDICROUS

MENACINGLY

MONOLOGUE

MUTILATED

OMINOUS

OPPRESSIVE

PENETRATED

PLAINTIVELY

PLUNDER

PRESUMABLY

PROPOSITION

REBUFFS

REVELATION

TENTATIVELY

TYRANT

VENGEANCE

VICIOUSLY

VINDICATED

WROUGHT

A Raisin in the Sun Vocabulary Crossword 1

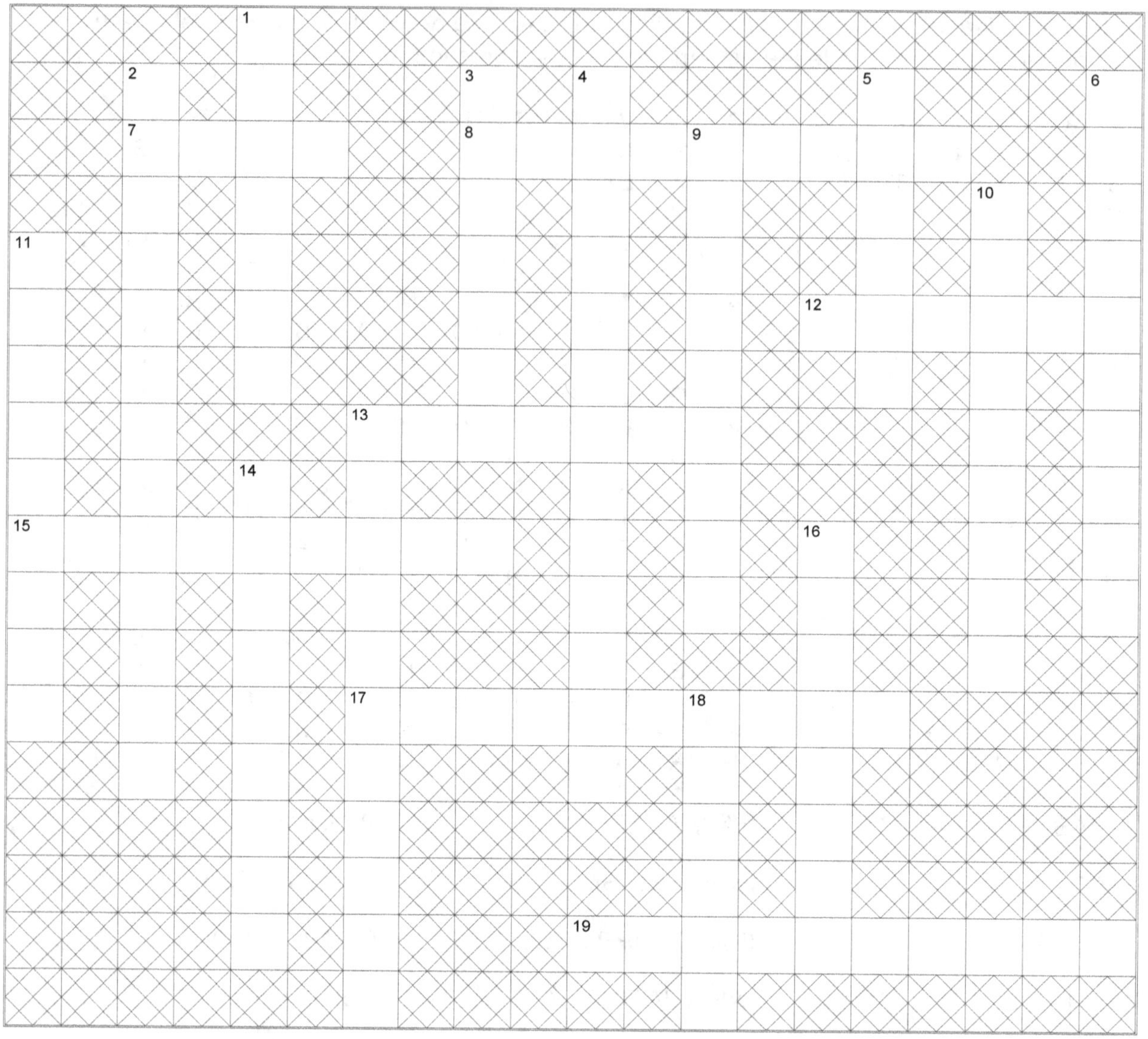

Across
7. Among; in the midst of
8. Long speech or talk made by one person
12. Trite or overused expression or idea
13. Hopelessness
15. Violently; maliciously
17. Some new information; news
19. Pierced; affected; diffused

Down
1. Good naturedly
2. In a manner using statements or implications opposite to the underlying meaning
3. Menacing; threatening
4. With more meaning than the spoken word; implying
5. Useless
6. Tyrannical
9. Laughably ridiculous
10. Deviating from the established norm, model or rule
11. Stealthily; expressive of hidden motives
13. Condition of being driven to take almost any risk as a last resort
14. Looking pitiful, desperate or hopeless
16. Overbearingly proud; haughty
18. Ruler who exercises power in a harsh, cruel manner

				1 A															
		2 S		M				3 O		4 I					5 F				6 O
		7 A	M	I	D			8 M	O	N	O	9 L	O	G	U	E			P
		R		A				I		S		U			T		10 E		P
11 F		C		B				N		I		D			I		C		R
U		A		L				O		N		I		12 C	L	I	C	H	E
R		S		Y				U		U		C			E		E		S
T		T				13 D	E	S	P	A	I	R					N		S
I		I		14 F		E				T		O					T		I
15 V	I	C	I	O	U	S	L	Y		I		U		16 A			R		V
E		A		R		P				N		S		R			I		E
L		L		L		E				G				R			C		
Y		L		O		17 R	E	V	E	L	A	18 T	I	O	N				
		Y		R		A				Y		Y		G					
				N		T						R		A					
				L		I						A		N					
				Y		O				19 P	E	N	E	T	R	A	T	E	D
						N						T							

Across
7. Among; in the midst of
8. Long speech or talk made by one person
12. Trite or overused expression or idea
13. Hopelessness
15. Violently; maliciously
17. Some new information; news
19. Pierced; affected; diffused

Down
1. Good naturedly
2. In a manner using statements or implications opposite to the underlying meaning
3. Menacing; threatening
4. With more meaning than the spoken word; implying
5. Useless
6. Tyrannical
9. Laughably ridiculous
10. Deviating from the established norm, model or rule
11. Stealthily; expressive of hidden motives
13. Condition of being driven to take almost any risk as a last resort
14. Looking pitiful, desperate or hopeless
16. Overbearingly proud; haughty
18. Ruler who exercises power in a harsh, cruel manner

A Raisin in the Sun Vocabulary Crossword 2

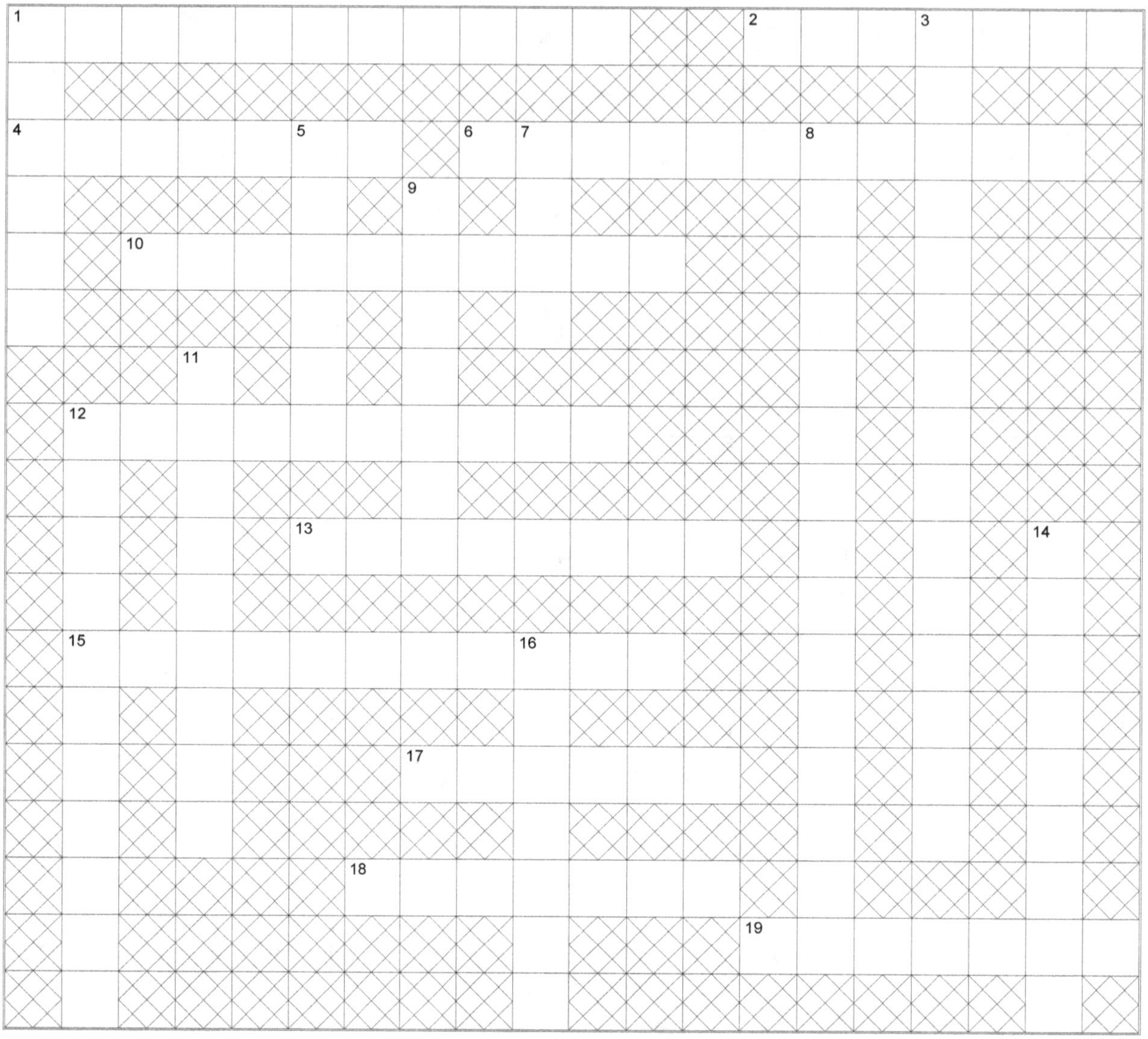

Across

1. Uncertainly
2. Shaped; made
4. Bluntly refuses
6. Without care; characterized by chance
10. Religion of those who don't beleive in God and/or are uncivilized
12. Having unrestrained high spirtis; being overjoyed
13. Overbearingly proud; haughty
15. Sorrowfully
17. Trite or overused expression or idea
18. Good naturedly
19. Menacing; threatening

Down

1. Ruler who exercises power in a harsh, cruel manner
3. Common; nothing special
5. Useless
7. Among; in the midst of
8. Belief that minority cultures should dissolve into a dominant culture
9. Hopelessness
11. Maimed; damaged
12. Irritated; provoked; irked
14. Laughably ridiculous
16. Inscription on a tombstone; summary of a deceased person's life

A Raisin in the Sun Vocabulary Crossword 2 Answer Key

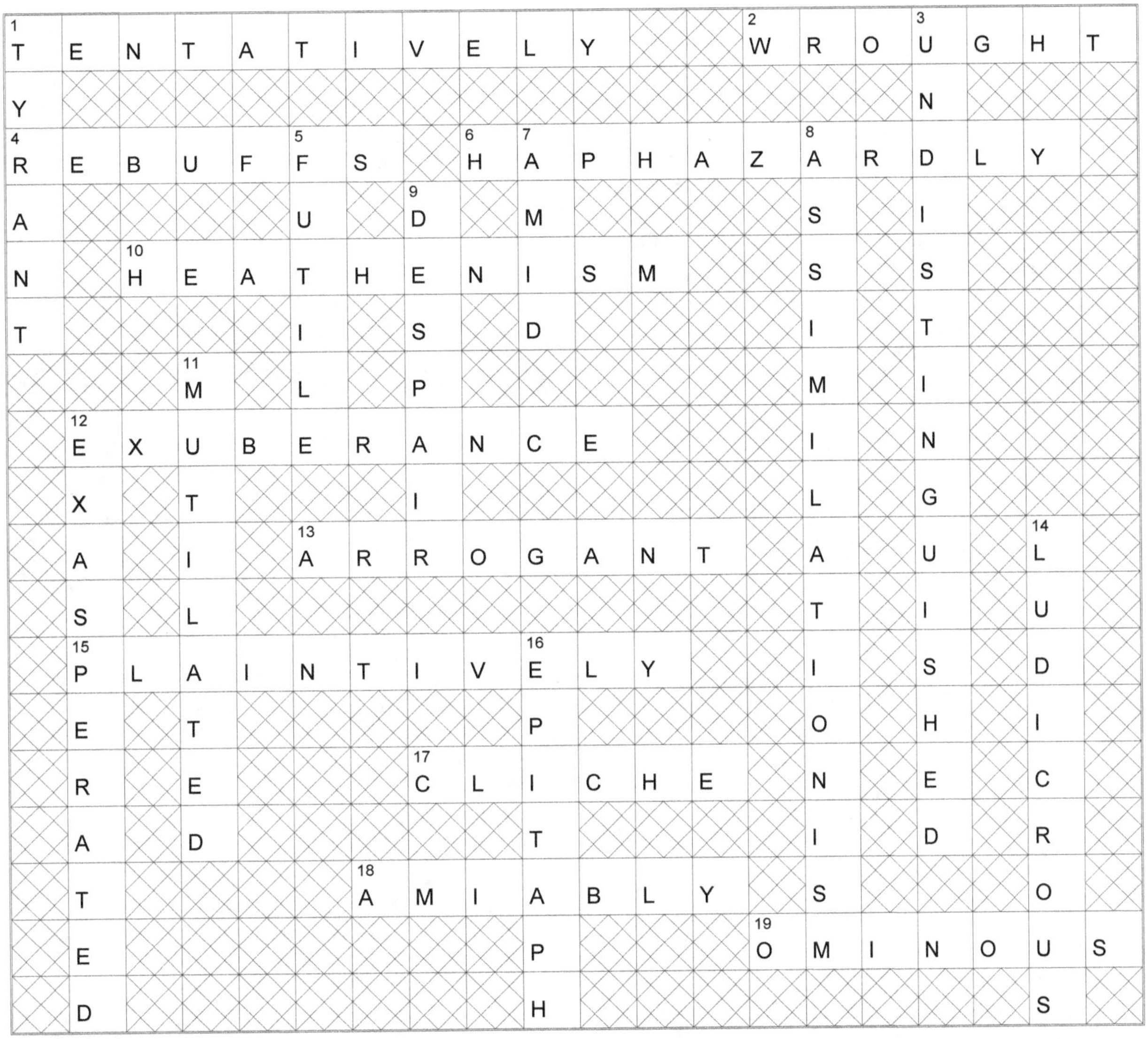

Across

1. Uncertainly
2. Shaped; made
4. Bluntly refuses
6. Without care; characterized by chance
10. Religion of those who don't beleive in God and/or are uncivilized
12. Having unrestrained high spirtis; being overjoyed
13. Overbearingly proud; haughty
15. Sorrowfully
17. Trite or overused expression or idea
18. Good naturedly
19. Menacing; threatening

Down

1. Ruler who exercises power in a harsh, cruel manner
3. Common; nothing special
5. Useless
7. Among; in the midst of
8. Belief that minority cultures should dissolve into a dominant culture
9. Hopelessness
11. Maimed; damaged
12. Irritated; provoked; irked
14. Laughably ridiculous
16. Inscription on a tombstone; summary of a deceased person's life

A Raisin in the Sun Vocabulary Crossword 3

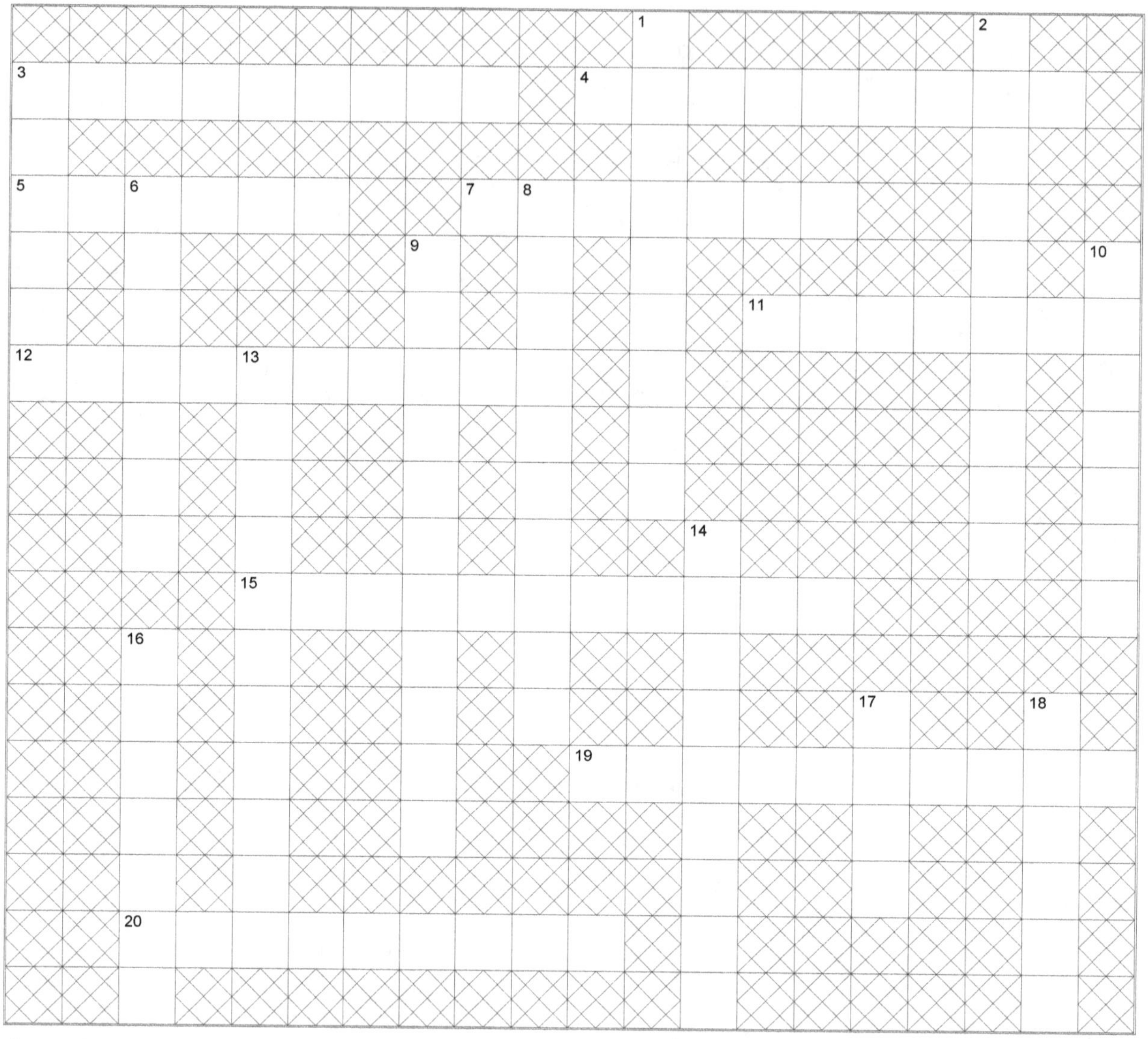

Across

3. Looking pitiful, desperate or hopeless
4. Maimed; damaged
5. Ruler who exercises power in a harsh, cruel manner
7. Inscription on a tombstone; summary of a deceased person's life
11. Hopelessness
12. Having unrestrained high spirtis; being overjoyed
15. Sorrowfully
19. Probably; reasonably supposed
20. Laughably ridiculous

Down

1. Stealthily; expressive of hidden motives
2. Some new information; news
3. Useless
6. Bluntly refuses
8. Pierced; affected; diffused
9. Uncertainly
10. Shaped; made
13. Irritated; provoked; irked
14. With violence or fury
16. Good naturedly
17. Among; in the midst of
18. Trite or overused expression or idea

A Raisin in the Sun Vocabulary Crossword 3 Answer Key

											1 F						2 R		
3 F	O	R	L	O	R	N	L	Y		4 M	U	T	I	L	A	T	E	D	
U											R						V		
5 T	Y	6 R	A	N	T			7 E	8 P	I	T	A	P	H			E		
I		E					9 T		E		I						L		10 W
L		B					E		N		V		11 D	E	S	P	A	I	R
12 E	X	U	B	13 E	R	A	N	C	E		E						T		O
		F		X			T		T		L						I		U
		F		A			A		R		Y						O		G
		S		S			T		A			14 V					N		H
				15 P	L	A	I	N	T	I	V	E	L	Y					T
		16 A		E			V		E			N							
		M		R			E		D			G			17 A			18 C	
		I		A			L			19 P	R	E	S	U	M	A	B	L	Y
		A		T			Y					A			I			I	
		B		E								N			D			C	
		20 L	U	D	I	C	R	O	U	S		C						H	
		Y										E						E	

Across
3. Looking pitiful, desperate or hopeless
4. Maimed; damaged
5. Ruler who exercises power in a harsh, cruel manner
7. Inscription on a tombstone; summary of a deceased person's life
11. Hopelessness
12. Having unrestrained high spirtis; being overjoyed
15. Sorrowfully
19. Probably; reasonably supposed
20. Laughably ridiculous

.

Down
1. Stealthily; expressive of hidden motives
2. Some new information; news
3. Useless
6. Bluntly refuses
8. Pierced; affected; diffused
9. Uncertainly
10. Shaped; made
13. Irritated; provoked; irked
14. With violence or fury
16. Good naturedly
17. Among; in the midst of
18. Trite or overused expression or idea

A Raisin in the Sun Vocabulary Crossword 4

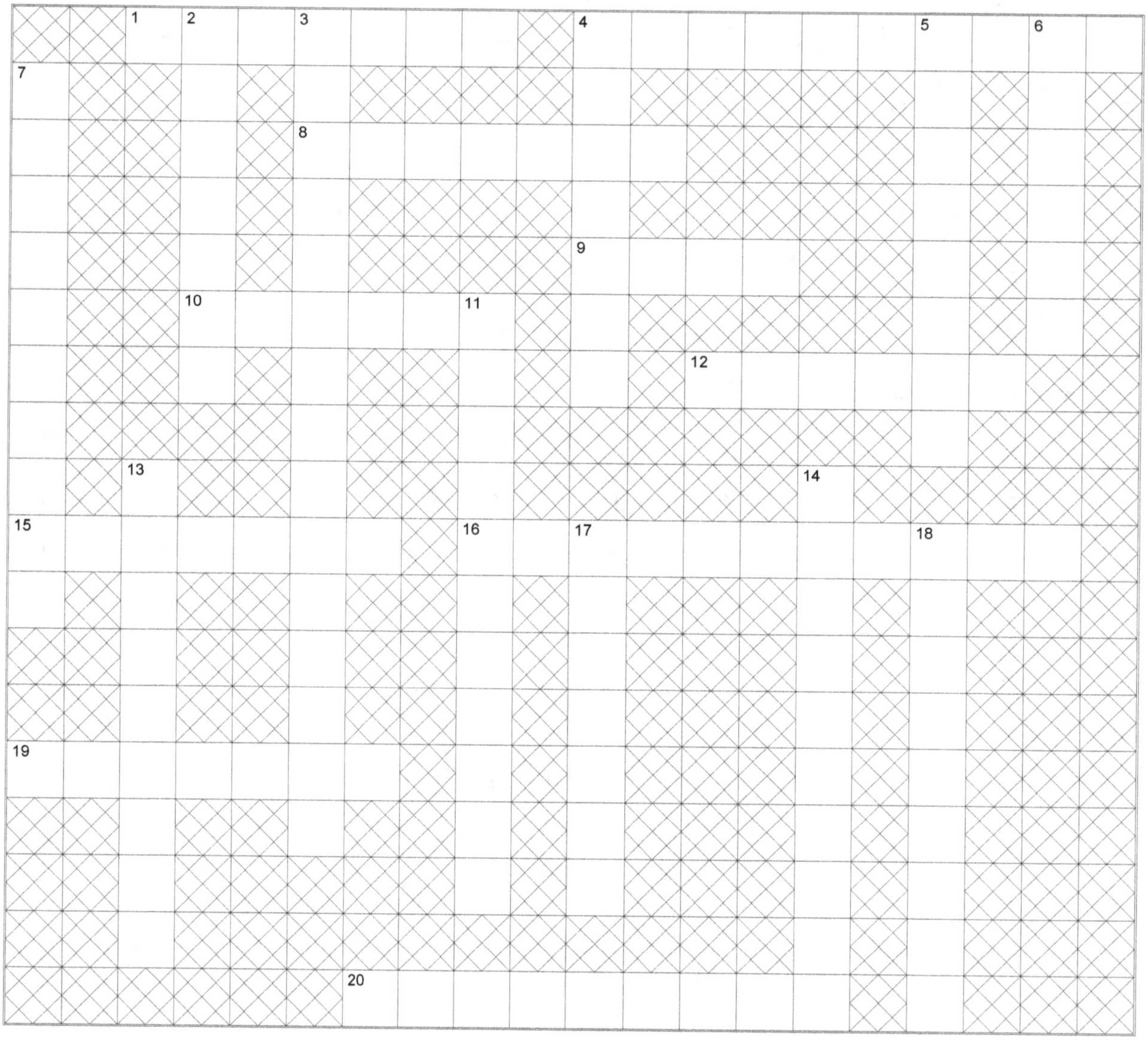

Across

1. Shaped; made
4. Having unrestrained high spirtis; being overjoyed
8. Hopelessness
9. Among; in the midst of
10. Useless
12. Ruler who exercises power in a harsh, cruel manner
15. Menacing; threatening
16. Sorrowfully
19. To rob of goods by force; loot
20. Maimed; damaged

Down

2. Bluntly refuses
3. Common; nothing special
4. Inscription on a tombstone; summary of a deceased person's life
5. Overbearingly proud; haughty
6. Trite or overused expression or idea
7. Some new information; news
11. Irritated; provoked; irked
13. Violently; maliciously
14. Cleared of accusations, blame or suspicion
17. Good naturedly
18. Deviating from the established norm, model or rule

A Raisin in the Sun Vocabulary Crossword 4 Answer Key

		1 W	2 R	O	3 U	G	H	T		4 E	X	U	B	E	R	5 A	N	6 C	E
7 R			E		N					P						R		L	
E			B		8 D	E	S	P	A	I	R					R		I	
V			U		I					T						O		C	
E			F		S					9 A	M	I	D			G		H	
L			10 F	U	T	I	L	11 E		P						A		E	
A			S		I			X		H		12 T	Y	R	A	N	T		
T					N			A								T			
I		13 V			G			S						14 V					
15 O	M	I	N	O	U	S		16 P	L	17 A	I	N	T	I	V	18 E	L	Y	
N		C			I			E		M				N		C			
		I			S			R		I				D		C			
		O			H			A		A				I		E			
19 P	L	U	N	D	E	R		T		B				C		N			
		S			D			E		L				A		T			
		L						D		Y				T		R			
		Y												E		I			
						20 M	U	T	I	L	A	T	E	D		C			

Across
1. Shaped; made
4. Having unrestrained high spirtis; being overjoyed
8. Hopelessness
9. Among; in the midst of
10. Useless
12. Ruler who exercises power in a harsh, cruel manner
15. Menacing; threatening
16. Sorrowfully
19. To rob of goods by force; loot
20. Maimed; damaged

.

Down
2. Bluntly refuses
3. Common; nothing special
4. Inscription on a tombstone; summary of a deceased person's life
5. Overbearingly proud; haughty
6. Trite or overused expression or idea
7. Some new information; news
11. Irritated; provoked; irked
13. Violently; maliciously
14. Cleared of accusations, blame or suspicion
17. Good naturedly
18. Deviating from the established norm, model or rule

A Raisin in the Sun Vocabulary Juggle Letters 1

1. LITFUE	= 1. ____________	Useless
2. OGTUHWR	= 2. ____________	Shaped; made
3. NOOGOLEMU	= 3. ____________	Long speech or talk made by one person
4. IDDEVACNTI	= 4. ____________	Cleared of accusations, blame or suspicion
5. ANMGCLNIEY	= 5. ____________	Threateningly
6. IFURVLYET	= 6. ____________	Stealthily; expressive of hidden motives
7. PVOISEPSER	= 7. ____________	Tyrannical
8. CVEANGEEN	= 8. ____________	With violence or fury
9. LAMYIAB	= 9. ____________	Good naturedly
10. ARPBEMYLSU	=10. ____________	Probably; reasonably supposed
11. URFFSEB	=11. ____________	Bluntly refuses
12. VNROTILEAE	=12. ____________	Some new information; news
13. DAIM	=13. ____________	Among; in the midst of
14. NEECXUBARE	=14. ____________	Having unrestrained high spirtis; being overjoyed
15. EEEAXTDSPAR	=15. ____________	Irritated; provoked; irked

A Raisin in the Sun Vocabulary Juggle Letters 1 Answer Key

1. LITFUE = 1. FUTILE
   Useless
2. OGTUHWR = 2. WROUGHT
   Shaped; made
3. NOOGOLEMU = 3. MONOLOGUE
   Long speech or talk made by one person
4. IDDEVACNTI = 4. VINDICATED
   Cleared of accusations, blame or suspicion
5. ANMGCLNIEY = 5. MENACINGLY
   Threateningly
6. IFURVLYET = 6. FURTIVELY
   Stealthily; expressive of hidden motives
7. PVOISEPSER = 7. OPPRESSIVE
   Tyrannical
8. CVEANGEEN = 8. VENGEANCE
   With violence or fury
9. LAMYIAB = 9. AMIABLY
   Good naturedly
10. ARPBEMYLSU =10. PRESUMABLY
   Probably; reasonably supposed
11. URFFSEB =11. REBUFFS
   Bluntly refuses
12. VNROTILEAE =12. REVELATION
   Some new information; news
13. DAIM =13. AMID
   Among; in the midst of
14. NEECXUBARE =14. EXUBERANCE
   Having unrestrained high spirtis; being overjoyed
15. EEEAXTDSPAR =15. EXASPERATED
   Irritated; provoked; irked

A Raisin in the Sun Vocabulary Juggle Letters 2

1. TTUQEYIHOSLC = 1. ____________________
In a manner befitting a woman who flirts with men

2. NCENEVEGA = 2. ____________________
With violence or fury

3. ASPYBUERML = 3. ____________________
Probably; reasonably supposed

4. PPHTEAI = 4. ____________________
Inscription on a tombstone; summary of a deceased person's life

5. NYATTR = 5. ____________________
Ruler who exercises power in a harsh, cruel manner

6. EYVRITFUL = 6. ____________________
Stealthily; expressive of hidden motives

7. DMAI = 7. ____________________
Among; in the midst of

8. YRONRLOLF = 8. ____________________
Looking pitiful, desperate or hopeless

9. RILAAAYSSCCTL = 9. ____________________
In a manner using statements or implications opposite to the underlying meaning

10. CICHLE =10. ____________________
Trite or overused expression or idea

11. YCIISLVUO =11. ____________________
Violently; maliciously

12. TTNPREEADE =12. ____________________
Pierced; affected; diffused

13. ROPALITNAPRYIEP =13. ____________________
Unsuitably; improperly

14. OCIUDSULR =14. ____________________
Laughably ridiculous

15. ITAMUDTLE =15. ____________________
Maimed; damaged

A Raisin in the Sun Vocabulary Juggle Letters 2 Answer Key

1. TTUQEYIHOSLC	= 1. COQUETTISHLY In a manner befitting a woman who flirts with men
2. NCENEVEGA	= 2. VENGEANCE With violence or fury
3. ASPYBUERML	= 3. PRESUMABLY Probably; reasonably supposed
4. PPHTEAI	= 4. EPITAPH Inscription on a tombstone; summary of a deceased person's life
5. NYATTR	= 5. TYRANT Ruler who exercises power in a harsh, cruel manner
6. EYVRITFUL	= 6. FURTIVELY Stealthily; expressive of hidden motives
7. DMAI	= 7. AMID Among; in the midst of
8. YRONRLOLF	= 8. FORLORNLY Looking pitiful, desperate or hopeless
9. RILAAAYSSCCTL	= 9. SARCASTICALLY In a manner using statements or implications opposite to the underlying meaning
10. CICHLE	=10. CLICHE Trite or overused expression or idea
11. YCIISLVUO	=11. VICIOUSLY Violently; maliciously
12. TTNPREEADE	=12. PENETRATED Pierced; affected; diffused
13. ROPALITNAPRYIEP	=13. INAPPROPRIATELY Unsuitably; improperly
14. OCIUDSULR	=14. LUDICROUS Laughably ridiculous
15. ITAMUDTLE	=15. MUTILATED Maimed; damaged

A Raisin in the Sun Vocabulary Juggle Letters 3

1. RRNYLLFOO = 1. ____________________
Looking pitiful, desperate or hopeless

2. MBLYIAA = 2. ____________________
Good naturedly

3. ETYLENIVATT = 3. ____________________
Uncertainly

4. LOPPYNRAIRITEAP = 4. ____________________
Unsuitably; improperly

5. UIYLTERVF = 5. ____________________
Stealthily; expressive of hidden motives

6. NDDATIECIV = 6. ____________________
Cleared of accusations, blame or suspicion

7. PAARDSXEEET = 7. ____________________
Irritated; provoked; irked

8. REATOLIVEN = 8. ____________________
Some new information; news

9. TNPIIYLALEV = 9. ____________________
Sorrowfully

10. FREBUSF =10. ____________________
Bluntly refuses

11. DAERTEPENT =11. ____________________
Pierced; affected; diffused

12. UCUOISRDL =12. ____________________
Laughably ridiculous

13. PPTEAHI =13. ____________________
Inscription on a tombstone; summary of a deceased person's life

14. CYVIULSIO =14. ____________________
Violently; maliciously

15. CYCRLSSTILAAA =15. ____________________
In a manner using statements or implications opposite to the underlying meaning

A Raisin in the Sun Vocabulary Juggle Letters 3 Answer Key

1. RRNYLLFOO	= 1. FORLORNLY Looking pitiful, desperate or hopeless
2. MBLYIAA	= 2. AMIABLY Good naturedly
3. ETYLENIVATT	= 3. TENTATIVELY Uncertainly
4. LOPPYNRAIRITEAP	= 4. INAPPROPRIATELY Unsuitably; improperly
5. UIYLTERVF	= 5. FURTIVELY Stealthily; expressive of hidden motives
6. NDDATIECIV	= 6. VINDICATED Cleared of accusations, blame or suspicion
7. PAARDSXEEET	= 7. EXASPERATED Irritated; provoked; irked
8. REATOLIVEN	= 8. REVELATION Some new information; news
9. TNPIIYLALEV	= 9. PLAINTIVELY Sorrowfully
10. FREBUSF	=10. REBUFFS Bluntly refuses
11. DAERTEPENT	=11. PENETRATED Pierced; affected; diffused
12. UCUOISRDL	=12. LUDICROUS Laughably ridiculous
13. PPTEAHI	=13. EPITAPH Inscription on a tombstone; summary of a deceased person's life
14. CYVIULSIO	=14. VICIOUSLY Violently; maliciously
15. CYCRLSSTILAAA	=15. SARCASTICALLY In a manner using statements or implications opposite to the underlying meaning

A Raisin in the Sun Vocabulary Juggle Letters 4

1. OORTIPNPOSI = 1. ____________________
Suggested plan

2. RRANGTAO = 2. ____________________
Overbearingly proud; haughty

3. SFUFEBR = 3. ____________________
Bluntly refuses

4. LAVEIPTILNY = 4. ____________________
Sorrowfully

5. EPDAISR = 5. ____________________
Hopelessness

6. BNAEREXUCE = 6. ____________________
Having unrestrained high spirtis; being overjoyed

7. SNEOETRIADP = 7. ____________________
Condition of being driven to take almost any risk as a last resort

8. ATERASXEPED = 8. ____________________
Irritated; provoked; irked

9. UGORTHW = 9. ____________________
Shaped; made

10. PITRRNOLIAAPPYE =10. ____________________
Unsuitably; improperly

11. HLZADYPAHAR =11. ____________________
Without care; characterized by chance

12. CEECRINTC =12. ____________________
Deviating from the established norm, model or rule

13. TISSIMMILNIOASA =13. ____________________
Belief that minority cultures should dissolve into a dominant culture

14. UDIOLSCRU =14. ____________________
Laughably ridiculous

15. AMLTUEITD =15. ____________________
Maimed; damaged

A Raisin in the Sun Vocabulary Juggle Letters 4 Answer Key

1. OORTIPNPOSI	= 1. PROPOSITION Suggested plan
2. RRANGTAO	= 2. ARROGANT Overbearingly proud; haughty
3. SFUFEBR	= 3. REBUFFS Bluntly refuses
4. LAVEIPTILNY	= 4. PLAINTIVELY Sorrowfully
5. EPDAISR	= 5. DESPAIR Hopelessness
6. BNAEREXUCE	= 6. EXUBERANCE Having unrestrained high spirtis; being overjoyed
7. SNEOETRIADP	= 7. DESPERATION Condition of being driven to take almost any risk as a last resort
8. ATERASXEPED	= 8. EXASPERATED Irritated; provoked; irked
9. UGORTHW	= 9. WROUGHT Shaped; made
10. PITRRNOLIAAPPYE	=10. INAPPROPRIATELY Unsuitably; improperly
11. HLZADYPAHAR	=11. HAPHAZARDLY Without care; characterized by chance
12. CEECRINTC	=12. ECCENTRIC Deviating from the established norm, model or rule
13. TISSIMMILNIOASA	=13. ASSIMILATIONISM Belief that minority cultures should dissolve into a dominant culture
14. UDIOLSCRU	=14. LUDICROUS Laughably ridiculous
15. AMLTUEITD	=15. MUTILATED Maimed; damaged

PLAINTIVELY	Sorrowfully
WROUGHT	Shaped; made
FUTILE	Useless
EXUBERANCE	Having unrestrained high spirtis; being overjoyed
REVELATION	Some new information; news
EXASPERATED	Irritated; provoked; irked

DESPAIR	Hopelessness
ASSIMILATIONISM	Belief that minority cultures should dissolve into a dominant culture
INAPPROPRIATELY	Unsuitably; improperly
HAPHAZARDLY	Without care; characterized by chance
MUTILATED	Maimed; damaged
ECCENTRIC	Deviating from the established norm, model or rule

HEATHENISM	Religion of those who don't beleive in God and/or are uncivilized
EPITAPH	Inscription on a tombstone; summary of a deceased person's life
PROPOSITION	Suggested plan
INSINUATINGLY	With more meaning than the spoken word; implying
VICIOUSLY	Violently; maliciously
CLICHE	Trite or overused expression or idea

UNDISTINGUISHED	Common; nothing special
LUDICROUS	Laughably ridiculous
ARROGANT	Overbearingly proud; haughty
TYRANT	Ruler who exercises power in a harsh, cruel manner
VINDICATED	Cleared of accusations, blame or suspicion
AMIABLY	Good naturedly

REBUFFS	Bluntly refuses
OPPRESSIVE	Tyrannical
COQUETTISHLY	In a manner befitting a woman who flirts with men
PENETRATED	Pierced; affected; diffused
PLUNDER	To rob of goods by force; loot
FORLORNLY	Looking pitiful, desperate or hopeless

PRESUMABLY	Probably; reasonably supposed
TENTATIVELY	Uncertainly
DESPERATION	Condition of being driven to take almost any risk as a last resort
MENACINGLY	Threateningly
SARCASTICALLY	In a manner using statements or implications opposite to the underlying meaning
VENGEANCE	With violence or fury

OMINOUS	Menacing; threatening
MONOLOGUE	Long speech or talk made by one person
AMID	Among; in the midst of
FURTIVELY	Stealthily; expressive of hidden motives

A Raisin in the Sun Vocabulary

VICIOUSLY	FURTIVELY	REBUFFS	TENTATIVELY	AMIABLY
CLICHE	FORLORNLY	INAPPROPRIATELY	EXASPERATED	PENETRATED
VENGEANCE	DESPERATION	FREE SPACE	FUTILE	TYRANT
HAPHAZARDLY	MENACINGLY	LUDICROUS	REVELATION	DESPAIR
ASSIMILATIONISM	SARCASTICALLY	UNDISTINGUISHED	COQUETTISHLY	PRESUMABLY

A Raisin in the Sun Vocabulary

EPITAPH	MUTILATED	PROPOSITION	VINDICATED	HEATHENISM
WROUGHT	PLAINTIVELY	OPPRESSIVE	INSINUATINGLY	MONOLOGUE
EXUBERANCE	ECCENTRIC	FREE SPACE	ARROGANT	AMID
PRESUMABLY	COQUETTISHLY	UNDISTINGUISHED	SARCASTICALLY	ASSIMILATIONISM
DESPAIR	REVELATION	LUDICROUS	MENACINGLY	HAPHAZARDLY

A Raisin in the Sun Vocabulary

AMIABLY	UNDISTINGUISHED	LUDICROUS	INSINUATINGLY	MUTILATED
VICIOUSLY	TYRANT	FORLORNLY	VENGEANCE	PLAINTIVELY
OMINOUS	PRESUMABLY	FREE SPACE	SARCASTICALLY	FURTIVELY
DESPERATION	OPPRESSIVE	ECCENTRIC	EXASPERATED	CLICHE
PROPOSITION	HAPHAZARDLY	HEATHENISM	EXUBERANCE	INAPPROPRIATELY

A Raisin in the Sun Vocabulary

WROUGHT	EPITAPH	FUTILE	MONOLOGUE	REBUFFS
DESPAIR	MENACINGLY	VINDICATED	PENETRATED	ARROGANT
COQUETTISHLY	ASSIMILATIONISM	FREE SPACE	TENTATIVELY	PLUNDER
INAPPROPRIATELY	EXUBERANCE	HEATHENISM	HAPHAZARDLY	PROPOSITION
CLICHE	EXASPERATED	ECCENTRIC	OPPRESSIVE	DESPERATION

A Raisin in the Sun Vocabulary

MENACINGLY	SARCASTICALLY	EXUBERANCE	OMINOUS	PENETRATED
VENGEANCE	AMIABLY	PRESUMABLY	OPPRESSIVE	DESPERATION
FORLORNLY	HEATHENISM	FREE SPACE	ASSIMILATIONISM	MONOLOGUE
TYRANT	DESPAIR	CLICHE	AMID	FUTILE
HAPHAZARDLY	ECCENTRIC	VINDICATED	TENTATIVELY	PLAINTIVELY

A Raisin in the Sun Vocabulary

COQUETTISHLY	REVELATION	VICIOUSLY	INSINUATINGLY	PLUNDER
UNDISTINGUISHED	FURTIVELY	MUTILATED	EXASPERATED	ARROGANT
INAPPROPRIATELY	REBUFFS	FREE SPACE	EPITAPH	LUDICROUS
PLAINTIVELY	TENTATIVELY	VINDICATED	ECCENTRIC	HAPHAZARDLY
FUTILE	AMID	CLICHE	DESPAIR	TYRANT

A Raisin in the Sun Vocabulary

FORLORNLY	PLUNDER	PRESUMABLY	FURTIVELY	VICIOUSLY
EXUBERANCE	VENGEANCE	OMINOUS	MUTILATED	AMID
ARROGANT	EPITAPH	FREE SPACE	UNDISTINGUISHED	EXASPERATED
DESPERATION	SARCASTICALLY	INAPPROPRIATELY	PROPOSITION	ASSIMILATIONISM
HAPHAZARDLY	COQUETTISHLY	DESPAIR	MONOLOGUE	ECCENTRIC

A Raisin in the Sun Vocabulary

TENTATIVELY	CLICHE	REBUFFS	LUDICROUS	INSINUATINGLY
PLAINTIVELY	REVELATION	VINDICATED	FUTILE	PENETRATED
MENACINGLY	HEATHENISM	FREE SPACE	WROUGHT	TYRANT
ECCENTRIC	MONOLOGUE	DESPAIR	COQUETTISHLY	HAPHAZARDLY
ASSIMILATIONISM	PROPOSITION	INAPPROPRIATELY	SARCASTICALLY	DESPERATION

A Raisin in the Sun Vocabulary

CLICHE	VINDICATED	DESPERATION	PROPOSITION	TYRANT
PLAINTIVELY	MONOLOGUE	REBUFFS	EXASPERATED	UNDISTINGUISHED
ASSIMILATIONISM	COQUETTISHLY	FREE SPACE	WROUGHT	SARCASTICALLY
PRESUMABLY	AMID	MUTILATED	REVELATION	INAPPROPRIATELY
VICIOUSLY	EPITAPH	AMIABLY	HEATHENISM	MENACINGLY

A Raisin in the Sun Vocabulary

OPPRESSIVE	INSINUATINGLY	ECCENTRIC	PENETRATED	HAPHAZARDLY
ARROGANT	LUDICROUS	OMINOUS	FURTIVELY	EXUBERANCE
TENTATIVELY	PLUNDER	FREE SPACE	VENGEANCE	FORLORNLY
MENACINGLY	HEATHENISM	AMIABLY	EPITAPH	VICIOUSLY
INAPPROPRIATELY	REVELATION	MUTILATED	AMID	PRESUMABLY

A Raisin in the Sun Vocabulary

PLUNDER	ASSIMILATIONISM	SARCASTICALLY	VINDICATED	VENGEANCE
COQUETTISHLY	UNDISTINGUISHED	MUTILATED	EPITAPH	EXASPERATED
PENETRATED	FUTILE	FREE SPACE	PLAINTIVELY	TYRANT
DESPAIR	PRESUMABLY	MENACINGLY	FURTIVELY	OPPRESSIVE
VICIOUSLY	TENTATIVELY	INSINUATINGLY	CLICHE	OMINOUS

A Raisin in the Sun Vocabulary

AMID	DESPERATION	INAPPROPRIATELY	AMIABLY	HEATHENISM
MONOLOGUE	WROUGHT	ARROGANT	REBUFFS	ECCENTRIC
EXUBERANCE	HAPHAZARDLY	FREE SPACE	LUDICROUS	PROPOSITION
OMINOUS	CLICHE	INSINUATINGLY	TENTATIVELY	VICIOUSLY
OPPRESSIVE	FURTIVELY	MENACINGLY	PRESUMABLY	DESPAIR

A Raisin in the Sun Vocabulary

OPPRESSIVE	COQUETTISHLY	FURTIVELY	INSINUATINGLY	OMINOUS
AMIABLY	TENTATIVELY	MONOLOGUE	MENACINGLY	REVELATION
ASSIMILATIONISM	CLICHE	FREE SPACE	FUTILE	INAPPROPRIATELY
DESPERATION	PROPOSITION	PENETRATED	PRESUMABLY	ECCENTRIC
WROUGHT	PLAINTIVELY	FORLORNLY	LUDICROUS	EPITAPH

A Raisin in the Sun Vocabulary

MUTILATED	REBUFFS	EXUBERANCE	PLUNDER	HEATHENISM
VICIOUSLY	VINDICATED	TYRANT	EXASPERATED	DESPAIR
ARROGANT	AMID	FREE SPACE	HAPHAZARDLY	VENGEANCE
EPITAPH	LUDICROUS	FORLORNLY	PLAINTIVELY	WROUGHT
ECCENTRIC	PRESUMABLY	PENETRATED	PROPOSITION	DESPERATION

A Raisin in the Sun Vocabulary

PRESUMABLY	OMINOUS	PLUNDER	AMID	TYRANT
REVELATION	LUDICROUS	SARCASTICALLY	MUTILATED	ECCENTRIC
WROUGHT	OPPRESSIVE	FREE SPACE	UNDISTINGUISHED	PLAINTIVELY
CLICHE	DESPAIR	EXASPERATED	MONOLOGUE	TENTATIVELY
COQUETTISHLY	PENETRATED	INAPPROPRIATELY	MENACINGLY	FUTILE

A Raisin in the Sun Vocabulary

ARROGANT	FORLORNLY	EXUBERANCE	VICIOUSLY	HAPHAZARDLY
FURTIVELY	VINDICATED	ASSIMILATIONISM	AMIABLY	PROPOSITION
VENGEANCE	INSINUATINGLY	FREE SPACE	DESPERATION	EPITAPH
FUTILE	MENACINGLY	INAPPROPRIATELY	PENETRATED	COQUETTISHLY
TENTATIVELY	MONOLOGUE	EXASPERATED	DESPAIR	CLICHE

A Raisin in the Sun Vocabulary

FORLORNLY	PRESUMABLY	OMINOUS	REBUFFS	VINDICATED
VICIOUSLY	DESPAIR	AMIABLY	AMID	TYRANT
WROUGHT	EPITAPH	FREE SPACE	HEATHENISM	FUTILE
PLUNDER	HAPHAZARDLY	MUTILATED	PLAINTIVELY	OPPRESSIVE
ECCENTRIC	ARROGANT	DESPERATION	CLICHE	EXASPERATED

A Raisin in the Sun Vocabulary

UNDISTINGUISHED	MONOLOGUE	EXUBERANCE	REVELATION	MENACINGLY
INSINUATINGLY	TENTATIVELY	COQUETTISHLY	FURTIVELY	LUDICROUS
PENETRATED	INAPPROPRIATELY	FREE SPACE	VENGEANCE	PROPOSITION
EXASPERATED	CLICHE	DESPERATION	ARROGANT	ECCENTRIC
OPPRESSIVE	PLAINTIVELY	MUTILATED	HAPHAZARDLY	PLUNDER

A Raisin in the Sun Vocabulary

ASSIMILATIONISM	DESPERATION	FORLORNLY	PROPOSITION	AMID
INSINUATINGLY	CLICHE	WROUGHT	HAPHAZARDLY	UNDISTINGUISHED
REBUFFS	EPITAPH	FREE SPACE	VINDICATED	PLAINTIVELY
ARROGANT	REVELATION	FUTILE	MENACINGLY	DESPAIR
AMIABLY	OPPRESSIVE	VICIOUSLY	TENTATIVELY	EXUBERANCE

A Raisin in the Sun Vocabulary

MUTILATED	SARCASTICALLY	TYRANT	PENETRATED	OMINOUS
PLUNDER	EXASPERATED	LUDICROUS	HEATHENISM	PRESUMABLY
COQUETTISHLY	FURTIVELY	FREE SPACE	INAPPROPRIATELY	VENGEANCE
EXUBERANCE	TENTATIVELY	VICIOUSLY	OPPRESSIVE	AMIABLY
DESPAIR	MENACINGLY	FUTILE	REVELATION	ARROGANT

A Raisin in the Sun Vocabulary

CLICHE	REBUFFS	AMID	VICIOUSLY	EPITAPH
DESPERATION	AMIABLY	INSINUATINGLY	ECCENTRIC	REVELATION
HAPHAZARDLY	COQUETTISHLY	FREE SPACE	MENACINGLY	UNDISTINGUISHED
VINDICATED	ASSIMILATIONISM	VENGEANCE	FORLORNLY	PRESUMABLY
EXUBERANCE	PLAINTIVELY	SARCASTICALLY	WROUGHT	MONOLOGUE

A Raisin in the Sun Vocabulary

TYRANT	PROPOSITION	LUDICROUS	ARROGANT	TENTATIVELY
OMINOUS	EXASPERATED	INAPPROPRIATELY	DESPAIR	OPPRESSIVE
FURTIVELY	MUTILATED	FREE SPACE	PLUNDER	HEATHENISM
MONOLOGUE	WROUGHT	SARCASTICALLY	PLAINTIVELY	EXUBERANCE
PRESUMABLY	FORLORNLY	VENGEANCE	ASSIMILATIONISM	VINDICATED

A Raisin in the Sun Vocabulary

ECCENTRIC	SARCASTICALLY	MUTILATED	HAPHAZARDLY	WROUGHT
INAPPROPRIATELY	FORLORNLY	PENETRATED	FURTIVELY	VICIOUSLY
PRESUMABLY	AMID	FREE SPACE	OPPRESSIVE	TENTATIVELY
TYRANT	REBUFFS	MENACINGLY	COQUETTISHLY	REVELATION
EPITAPH	PLUNDER	ASSIMILATIONISM	CLICHE	FUTILE

A Raisin in the Sun Vocabulary

AMIABLY	DESPAIR	PROPOSITION	VENGEANCE	VINDICATED
UNDISTINGUISHED	MONOLOGUE	EXUBERANCE	DESPERATION	PLAINTIVELY
OMINOUS	INSINUATINGLY	FREE SPACE	ARROGANT	LUDICROUS
FUTILE	CLICHE	ASSIMILATIONISM	PLUNDER	EPITAPH
REVELATION	COQUETTISHLY	MENACINGLY	REBUFFS	TYRANT

A Raisin in the Sun Vocabulary

HEATHENISM	ARROGANT	FORLORNLY	PLAINTIVELY	FURTIVELY
ECCENTRIC	INSINUATINGLY	COQUETTISHLY	AMIABLY	MENACINGLY
DESPERATION	DESPAIR	FREE SPACE	WROUGHT	FUTILE
REVELATION	SARCASTICALLY	OMINOUS	EXASPERATED	EPITAPH
UNDISTINGUISHED	TYRANT	HAPHAZARDLY	MONOLOGUE	TENTATIVELY

A Raisin in the Sun Vocabulary

AMID	PROPOSITION	INAPPROPRIATELY	VICIOUSLY	PENETRATED
CLICHE	OPPRESSIVE	EXUBERANCE	REBUFFS	MUTILATED
PRESUMABLY	PLUNDER	FREE SPACE	ASSIMILATIONISM	LUDICROUS
TENTATIVELY	MONOLOGUE	HAPHAZARDLY	TYRANT	UNDISTINGUISHED
EPITAPH	EXASPERATED	OMINOUS	SARCASTICALLY	REVELATION

A Raisin in the Sun Vocabulary

EXASPERATED	MUTILATED	ASSIMILATIONISM	HEATHENISM	LUDICROUS
PLAINTIVELY	INSINUATINGLY	VICIOUSLY	FUTILE	DESPAIR
CLICHE	FORLORNLY	FREE SPACE	COQUETTISHLY	INAPPROPRIATELY
MONOLOGUE	UNDISTINGUISHED	HAPHAZARDLY	VENGEANCE	ECCENTRIC
AMIABLY	PROPOSITION	SARCASTICALLY	ARROGANT	PRESUMABLY

A Raisin in the Sun Vocabulary

TENTATIVELY	TYRANT	EXUBERANCE	REBUFFS	FURTIVELY
PENETRATED	MENACINGLY	EPITAPH	OMINOUS	VINDICATED
OPPRESSIVE	DESPERATION	FREE SPACE	AMID	WROUGHT
PRESUMABLY	ARROGANT	SARCASTICALLY	PROPOSITION	AMIABLY
ECCENTRIC	VENGEANCE	HAPHAZARDLY	UNDISTINGUISHED	MONOLOGUE

A Raisin in the Sun Vocabulary

HEATHENISM	CLICHE	FORLORNLY	PLUNDER	EPITAPH
REVELATION	DESPERATION	VINDICATED	PROPOSITION	PLAINTIVELY
VICIOUSLY	INSINUATINGLY	FREE SPACE	HAPHAZARDLY	AMIABLY
MUTILATED	PENETRATED	REBUFFS	OPPRESSIVE	FUTILE
EXASPERATED	PRESUMABLY	WROUGHT	TYRANT	MONOLOGUE

A Raisin in the Sun Vocabulary

TENTATIVELY	ECCENTRIC	EXUBERANCE	SARCASTICALLY	MENACINGLY
FURTIVELY	UNDISTINGUISHED	LUDICROUS	VENGEANCE	COQUETTISHLY
OMINOUS	DESPAIR	FREE SPACE	INAPPROPRIATELY	AMID
MONOLOGUE	TYRANT	WROUGHT	PRESUMABLY	EXASPERATED
FUTILE	OPPRESSIVE	REBUFFS	PENETRATED	MUTILATED

A Raisin in the Sun Vocabulary

PROPOSITION	SARCASTICALLY	AMIABLY	LUDICROUS	INSINUATINGLY
CLICHE	EXUBERANCE	UNDISTINGUISHED	MUTILATED	ECCENTRIC
REVELATION	PLUNDER	FREE SPACE	OPPRESSIVE	COQUETTISHLY
PENETRATED	PRESUMABLY	OMINOUS	FURTIVELY	EXASPERATED
VINDICATED	TYRANT	VICIOUSLY	DESPAIR	AMID

A Raisin in the Sun Vocabulary

PLAINTIVELY	WROUGHT	EPITAPH	INAPPROPRIATELY	MENACINGLY
HAPHAZARDLY	HEATHENISM	MONOLOGUE	ARROGANT	FORLORNLY
ASSIMILATIONISM	FUTILE	FREE SPACE	VENGEANCE	REBUFFS
AMID	DESPAIR	VICIOUSLY	TYRANT	VINDICATED
EXASPERATED	FURTIVELY	OMINOUS	PRESUMABLY	PENETRATED

www.ingramcontent.com/pod-product-compliance
Lightning Source LLC
Chambersburg PA
CBHW081456070526
44586CB00019B/2381
9781602493926